Ulysses S. Grant

A Captivating Guide to the American General Who Served as the 18th President of the United States of America

© Copyright 2022

All Rights Reserved. No part of this book may be reproduced in any form without permission in writing from the author. Reviewers may quote brief passages in reviews.

Disclaimer: No part of this publication may be reproduced or transmitted in any form or by any means, mechanical or electronic, including photocopying or recording, or by any information storage and retrieval system, or transmitted by email without permission in writing from the publisher.

While all attempts have been made to verify the information provided in this publication, neither the author nor the publisher assumes any responsibility for errors, omissions or contrary interpretations of the subject matter herein.

This book is for entertainment purposes only. The views expressed are those of the author alone, and should not be taken as expert instruction or commands. The reader is responsible for his or her own actions.

Adherence to all applicable laws and regulations, including international, federal, state and local laws governing professional licensing, business practices, advertising and all other aspects of doing business in the US, Canada, UK or any other jurisdiction is the sole responsibility of the purchaser or reader.

Neither the author nor the publisher assumes any responsibility or liability whatsoever on the behalf of the purchaser or reader of these materials. Any perceived slight of any individual or organization is purely unintentional.

Free Bonus from Captivating History (Available for a Limited time)

Hi History Lovers!

Now you have a chance to join our exclusive history list so you can get your first history ebook for free as well as discounts and a potential to get more history books for free! Simply visit the link below to join.

Captivatinghistory.com/ebook

Also, make sure to follow us on Facebook, Twitter and Youtube by searching for Captivating History.

Contents

INTRODUCTION - HE WAS A GENERAL, A GENTLEMAN, AND A SCHOLAR–AND HE ALSO HAPPENED TO BE THE 18TH PRESIDENT 1
CHAPTER 1 - FROM GEORGETOWN TO WEST POINT 3
CHAPTER 2 - GRADUATION AND THE FIRST CALL OF DUTY 12
CHAPTER 3 - HEADED OFF TO WAR 19
CHAPTER 4 - GRANT'S LONELY OUTPOST 28
CHAPTER 5 - LIVING A HARDSCRABBLE LIFE 37
CHAPTER 6 - THE CIVIL WAR BEGINS 42
CHAPTER 7 - READY FOR ANYTHING 49
CHAPTER 8 - THE BATTLE OF SHILOH AND ITS AFTERMATH 54
CHAPTER 9 - THE TAKING OF VICKSBURG 60
CHAPTER 10 - THE CIVIL WAR COMES TO AN END 68
CHAPTER 11 - GRANT'S ROLE AS LINCOLN'S SUCCESSOR 78
CONCLUSION: THE PURSUIT OF PERFECTION 88
HERE'S ANOTHER BOOK BY CAPTIVATING HISTORY THAT YOU MIGHT LIKE 91
FREE BONUS FROM CAPTIVATING HISTORY (AVAILABLE FOR A LIMITED TIME) 92
APPENDIX A: FURTHER READING AND REFERENCES 93

Introduction – He Was a General, a Gentleman, and a Scholar—and He Also Happened to be the 18th President

People in the United States see his face staring up at them from the $50 bill. Printed on this pale green material, Grant looks stoic, if not a bit uncomfortable. In fact, a bit of aloofness and a chronic sense of restlessness was a permanent feature of this former president and general.

Ulysses S. Grant is often remembered in heroic terms. And rightly enough. He was a man whose courage managed to command respect even from his enemies, both on the battlefield and in the political arena. Even so, as with many legendary figures, layers of embellishment built up over the years that cover the real man.

Grant certainly was not perfect. He tended to be overly sensitive and had bouts of melancholy at times. An acute episode of depression actually led Grant to drop out of the military as a young man. It would take several years of hardship and the eruption of the Civil War to get Grant reinstated.

Grant's temperament could indeed be unpredictable at times, but the great thing about Ulysses S. Grant was his determination. Once there was a task at hand, he knew he would complete it. Grant knew, for example, that the North would ultimately win the Civil War. He knew that it was just a matter of national endurance to see the war through to the end.

Grant was ultimately a man of action; he could not stand the feeling of listless idleness. He did not mind putting out fires, and he happily moved from one complex issue to the next. On the contrary, it was sitting and waiting with nothing to do that Grant disliked. It was perhaps for this reason that this two-term president came to dislike the presidency so much in his later years.

For Grant, the presidency was far too ephemeral for his tastes. He knew that much of his work in politics could be easily undone by others. After realizing the transitory nature of the presidency, he would ultimately decline what would have been a third term. Nevertheless, he has gone down as a man of the ages. Here is the story of that stoic figure on the $50 bill—here is the story of Ulysses S. Grant.

Chapter 1 – From Georgetown to West Point

"Nations, like individuals, are punished for their transgressions."
   -Ulysses S. Grant

Ulysses S. Grant was a product of what was at that time the still rugged frontier country of Ohio. He was the son of a man by the name of Jesse Root Grant. The elder Grant was known as a no-nonsense craftsman who worked with his hands and led with his heart. He was a tanner by trade, producing leather goods such as shoes and saddles. As an ambitious and driven young man, Jesse caught the attention of one Hannah Simpson.

After a whirlwind courtship, the couple married, and it was from this union that Ulysses S. Grant was born on April 27th, 1822. Grant's full name at birth was actually Hiram Ulysses Grant. His family tended to simply call him Ulysses and sometimes even by the shortened variation of "Lyss." In later years, Grant would drop Hiram altogether and just go by Ulysses. Many might wonder then where the "S" in Ulysses S. Grant comes from? That was actually the product of a typo.

We are getting a bit ahead of the chronological narrative of Grant's life, but in order to avoid confusion, this story is worth telling at the beginning. The incident occurred when Ulysses was seeking admittance to West Point. He received a recommendation from an Ohio congressman by the name of Thomas Hamer. It was Hamer who accidentally printed Ulysses's full name as being "Ulysses S. Grant."

In reality, there is no "S" in Ulysses's name, so therefore the "S" does not stand for anything at all. After his successful acceptance at West Point, Ulysses discovered that the name "Ulysses S. Grant" had stuck, and he just went with it for the rest of his life. Now with that little aside out of the way, let us take a look at the early days of the man we have come to know as Ulysses S. Grant.

He was the oldest child in his family, although many siblings would follow him. His brother Samuel was born in 1825, and he had a sister Clara in 1828. Another sister named Virginia popped up in 1832, then a brother named Orvil in 1835, and finally one more little sister by the name of Mary in 1839. Ulysses and his brothers and sisters grew up in the cozy confines of Georgetown, Ohio.

Grant first attended school at the age of five. It was one of those classic one-room schoolhouses that became so ubiquitous on the frontier. It may have had its rustic charms, but his lessons certainly were not free. His parents dutifully paid the yearly fee so that their children could go to school. The school lessons, as one might expect in those days, consisted of basic reading, writing, and arithmetic.

It was nothing too in-depth, just the basics of knowing how to read, sign one's name, and add and subtract. It was the latter that the young Ulysses seemed to excel. His quick mind always outdid his peers when it came to shouting out the answers to math problems. Even so, his school year was very short in duration, purportedly only stretching throughout the winter months. Ulysses would be back at home helping his parents with various household chores as soon as spring arrived.

Back on the old homestead, Grant, like many other children of his time and place, became proficient with firearms. However, the interesting thing about Grant was the fact that while other young men developed their abilities with the rifle, Grant was always keen to practice his luck with a handgun. Since hunting—the primary goal of becoming a good shot in the backwoods—was not done with handguns, this was a bit unusual. But nevertheless, Grant became a good marksman.

Along with his education and ability as a skilled marksman, Grant was an avid lover of horses and had developed a finely honed level of horsemanship. It has been said that Grant rode horses ever since he was a little boy. Ulysses was especially good at calming wild and unruly horses, which is a great skill to have in an age when so much depended upon horse travel. His abilities can be demonstrated from one tale of his youth. It was said that he had a new untamed horse leading him in a buggy when the steed suddenly decided to bolt.

The horse was unresponsive to the reins, and it took Grant on a wild ride across the countryside. As the story goes, the horse nearly led Grant off the edge of a steep cliff. The animal managed to stop, and the quick-thinking Ulysses had an idea. He took a bandana and wrapped it around the maddened horse's eyes. As strange as this might sound, the darkness of not being able to see calmed the spooked horse. Grant was able to lead the now blinded animal back home merely by his own direction on the reins.

It is said that Ulysses purchased his first horse at the age of nine. He had worked part-time hauling wood, and he was ready to use his earnings to get a horse of his own. The story in itself provides us with an amusing anecdote of a young man eager to buy a horse. However, he was not well-versed in negotiating.

His father had apparently tried to haggle with the seller on the price, offering $20, but the seller refused. Ulysses's father instructed his son to go to the seller and try to offer $20 himself to see what the seller might do. His dad advised him that if the seller again refused to then offer $22.50. If he refused this amount, then Ulysses should tell him that he was willing to pay as much as $25. This is pretty sound advice for negotiating a business deal, but the naïve Ulysses ended up showing his cards.

The seller point-blank asked him, "How much did your father tell you to pay?" To which Ulysses steadfastly replied, "Papa says I may offer you $20 for the colt, but if you won't take that, I am to offer $22.50. And if you won't take that, to give you $25." With perhaps a chuckle or two of surprise, the wily seller cut the negotiations short by informing the young man that he could not possibly accept anything less than $25.

Ulysses got his horse, but the details of the deal were passed around to other locals, and soon his peers were laughing at his expense. Ulysses was likened to being a simpleton, and they began to tease Grant by calling him "Useless" Grant. This ridicule deeply affected Grant, and he would have a tendency to be quite sensitive to any form of mockery leveled at him in the future.

As he grew older, Grant expressed his dislike of working at his father's tannery. It was a laborious, often gruesome business, after all, which involved soaking animal skins in lime. And the tedious work of plucking out hair certainly was not pleasant. His abilities with horses won him a way out, as Grant would be the one responsible for loading up his saddle with his father's latest goods and taking them to market.

He would also equip his horses with a buggy and chauffeur people back and forth, offering rides to paying customers and taking them as far away as Chillicothe, Ohio, which was some sixty miles away. These travels when he was just a young man would give Ulysses a sense of the larger world around him. Many believe that it was his days as a horse chauffer that instilled in him a desire to see lands far removed from his familiar family homestead.

Jesse, by all accounts, was proud of his son. When Ulysses was a young boy, Jesse would profess that his eldest child was destined for great things. And according to one tantalizing anecdote, Jesse was not the only one. It has been said that on one occasion, a visiting phrenologist declared as much as well.

Phrenologists were infamous in the 19th century for supposedly gleaning the standout characteristics of people through their physical features. They were sort of like the 19th-century version of a fortune teller and chiropractor combined. Phrenologists felt around on people's heads, necks, and shoulders to try and decipher what a person was like.

This particular phrenologist is said to have studied the young Ulysses intently. After taking a look at his head shape, he came away absolutely delighted. The phrenologist solemnly proclaimed, "It is no very common head! It is an extraordinary head!"

As Jesse and his son stared in wonder, the man then added, "It would not be strange if we should see him President of the United States!" Most today would probably assume this man was just out to make a quick buck from a parent like Jesse who was eager to pay to hear such good news. There likely was nothing "extraordinary" about Grant's head, especially since phrenology has been deemed a pseudoscience today. But perhaps his words planted a seed in Ulysses's mind. As most of us know, Ulysses S. Grant was indeed destined to become a US president.

Shortly after the phrenologist's proclamation, in 1836, the budding Ulysses Grant, then fourteen years old, was delivered to Maysville, Kentucky, to attend seminary school. Here, he found himself somewhat disenchanted with the curriculum, which did not seem much more challenging than what he had learned in the single-room schoolhouse back home. He did manage to get involved with a debate team, which allowed him to stimulate his mind. He debated the important topics of the day, such as ending slavery and whether or not the newly independent territory of Texas should be admitted to the Union.

Ulysses Grant would return home to Georgetown by the time spring had arrived. He would reach a turning point in his young life when he finally let his father know that he did not intend to follow him into the tanning business. This frank discussion occurred in the summer of 1838 after Ulysses was forced to help his father out with his work. Ulysses was made to stretch hides over beams and scrape hair from the skins.

In the midst of this work, which Ulysses found incredibly distasteful, he told his father that his mind was made up. He remarked to his dear old dad, "Father, this tanning is not the kind of work I like. I'll work at it, though, if you wish me to, until I am twenty-one. But you may depend on it, I'll never work a day at it after that." His father was surprisingly lenient with Ulysses, considering the harshness of the time in which parents were often strict enforcers of their will.

His dad is said to have told his son, "I want you to work at whatever you like and intend to follow. Now, what do you think you like?" Ulysses admitted that there were three paths he was thinking about taking. He explained to his father that he could see himself either being a trader, a farmer, or simply going on to further his education by attending college.

Farming was a noble enterprise, and it was one that Grant respected. However, it would have made the young man stationary. He did not desire to stay in one place, so he considered becoming a trader, making a living trading goods on a riverboat going up and down the Mississippi. It would have been a profitable enough enterprise, but traders tended to be unstable socially. Many of them had a penchant for drinking, gambling, and womanizing. Ulysses knew his parents would not enjoy such a prospect.

His parents were staunch Methodists, but they were surprisingly lenient with their son when it came to church. He was never forced to go to church on Sunday if he did not want to, and Grant would largely remain agnostic for much of his life.

And he was not only agnostic with religion in those days; he was also agnostic with politics.

In today's polarizing times, in which almost everyone seems to take one side or the other, it may be hard for us to imagine. However, as a young man, Grant did not have any real political leanings. He just lived his life and left politics to others. Interestingly enough, although Grant, who is often viewed as the true successor of Abraham Lincoln, would one day become a Republican president, it was a Democrat who paved the way for the furtherance of Grant's education.

In 1839, a seventeen-year-old Grant sought to enroll at West Point to become an officer. His father Jesse had lobbied a Democrat congressman by the name of Thomas L. Hamer for aid in securing Grant's enrollment. Hamer represented the Grant family's district in Ohio. Jesse contacted the congressman and saw to it that he recommended his son for enrollment at West Point.

Jesse was the one who came up with the whole idea, thinking that West Point would give Grant the higher education he desired. And if he was accepted, the US government would even foot the bill. The ploy worked. After Grant passed the entrance exam, he was duly enrolled that fall. As mentioned above, the helpful Congressman Hamer accidentally referred to the new young cadet as "Ulysses S. Grant" in his entrance papers—thereby branding him for life with a meaningless middle initial.

Grant had to remain at a boarding facility filled with West Point applicants for two weeks before he received word that he had passed the test. Once cleared, he was then off to get a haircut and get fitted for a uniform. Here, Grant was utterly amazed at the work of Joe the barber, who was able to cut down a new recruit's hair to virtually nothing all with just a pair of scissors. These were the days before electronic clippers, so the fact that this man was able to cut their hair down to just stubble atop their head must have truly been impressive.

After that, these clean-cut recruits headed off to the barracks of West Point. Upon their arrival, the greatest hurdle they faced was the older students, who mercilessly teased these new recruits as soon as they saw them. Another humiliation was the fact that it was a custom to teach the new cadets how to dance. The idea of teaching soldiers ballroom dancing might seem a bit ridiculous today, and the fact that the school forced these awkward young men to dance together made it all the more absurd.

Nevertheless, on September 14th, 1839, Grant made his commitments clear. He signed his official documents of enlistment, with the words, "I, Cadet U.S. Grant do hereby engage, with the consent of my guardian, to serve in the Army of the United States for eight years, unless sooner discharged by the proper authority." It was with these solemn words that Grant had committed himself to the austere life of the West Point Barracks.

His days would begin early, at around five in the morning. He would be woken up to the sound of the military drum roll, which served as an alarm clock. Ulysses Grant is said to have developed a distaste for loud music. Many believe that it likely stems from these rude awakenings, with this blaring martial, military music. The drum beats woke him up and then accompanied him to class, and he heard them once again before he went to sleep at night.

Nevertheless, Grant was determined to make it—drumming and all. And he was not only going to make it; he was going to grow to like it. This was evidenced by a letter he wrote back home to a cousin of his shortly into his stay. In it, he had suddenly become surprisingly upbeat. The young cadet penned, "West point is decidedly the most beautiful place I have ever seen. From the window near by [sic] I can see the Hudson...Its bosom studded with hundreds of snow white sails...On the whole I would not go away on any account. The fact is if a man graduates here he is safer fer [sic] life. Let him go where he will. There is much to dislike but more to like. I mean to study hard and stay if possible. Contrary to you and the rest of my friends I have not been the least homesick—no!"

He was a fairly popular cadet by the recollection of most who knew him. And those who did would recall that the young man was often called "Uncle Sam" or sometimes just "Sam" due to his first two initials being "U. S." But not everyone was always so kind to Grant.

In one instance, which historians have often retold, he was severely tested by a bigger cadet who decided to try his luck bullying Grant. According to the story, Grant was simply in line at the mess hall, waiting to get his food just like everyone else, when fellow cadet Jack Lindsay suddenly shoved him out of the line, as if he were going to take his place.

Grant, who was used to talking his way out of problems back home, was surprisingly patient with the uncouth youth, telling him to simply be more careful in the future. But when Lindsay tried to shove Grant again, all hell broke loose. An animalistic rage erupted from Grant, and he leaped upon his tormenter, knocking him to the ground.

Grant then began pummeling his foe with his hammer-like mitts. His hands were indeed iron-strong from his many years of helping his dad tan hides, as well as his many hours controlling wild horses. As such, Grant, even though he was smaller than this blowhard bully, was able to make short work of him. Lindsay was beaten so badly that from that day forward, no one messed with Ulysses S. Grant. He would be allowed to eat in the mess hall in peace.

Chapter 2 – Graduation and the First Call of Duty

"There never was a time when, in my opinion, some way could not be found to prevent the drawing of the sword."

-Ulysses S. Grant

After two years at West Point, Grant was given the customary sixty-day leave that was given to second-year students. He took this time to head home to his folks in Ohio. His family had since moved to the town of Bethel, which was about ten miles away from Georgetown.

In May of 1841, this young cadet was seen getting off a stagecoach near Bethel and then paying a local driver to transport him the rest of his journey by horse-drawn buggy. Upon dropping off this elegantly clad young man in his crisp West Point uniform, the driver figured his family would come rushing out to greet him. This was not the case.

Ulysses S. Grant was known later in life as being a fairly reserved fellow, and his family was of a similar disposition. Instead of rushing out to say how much they missed him and how glad they were to see him, his family delivered characteristic flatline responses. His mother and father simply asked, "How are you, son?" And likewise, his younger siblings simply inquired, "How are you, brother?"

At any rate, after this slight reprieve with his folks, Grant was back at West Point to finish the rest of his tenure at the school. Upon his return, he was promoted to the rank of sergeant in the Corps of Cadets. His greatest challenge in finishing up what remained of his coursework was math. Grant had been quite good at general mathematics during his elementary education back in Ohio, but he found higher mathematics, such as algebra, more challenging.

Nevertheless, he not only cracked the secret to succeeding in algebra but also excelled in geometry, trigonometry, and calculus. With higher math conquered, there was nothing left to hold this cadet back.

At West Point, Grant also carried on his passion for horse riding, and he became known as a proficient horseman by his peers. This was important since being able to serve as an officer in the cavalry was a big deal. Grant's most legendary exploits were with a rough and tumble horse called York.

This was a big animal, and it was said to be difficult to control, save for the best riders. Grant was intrigued, and he made it his mission to tame this beast. And tame it he did. With this belligerent beast of burden, Grant managed to surpass the high-jump record. Grant's feat would not be surpassed for another twenty-five years at the institution.

However, not all of Grant's exploits were as admirable. And as good as he was with horses, it has been said that during his senior year, in March of 1843, there was an instance in which he became so agitated with a horse that he actually gave it a good, solid whack with his saber. Such careless violence from an officer against a horse was considered highly improper. Grant's actions caused him to be punished with what amounted to house arrest—two weeks of seclusion in the barracks.

Nevertheless, he persevered and got through these hard times. Ulysses S. Grant ended up finishing his time at West Point in 1843, and he attended his official graduation ceremony on June 30th of that year. Once he graduated, though, Grant had to figure out what to do next. He went back to Bethel, and shortly after his arrival, he received news from Washington that he had received a commission to be a brevet second lieutenant in the 4th Infantry Regiment. He would soon be posted at the Jefferson Barracks in Missouri.

In the meantime, Grant had some catching up to do back home. He was now a military man, and just the sight of his sharp uniform, with its trim blue, white, and gold fittings, was enough to command attention. But not everyone was so generous—in fact, they maybe were even jealous. At one point during an outing in Cincinnati, a youngster approached Grant. He took one look at his fine uniform and shouted, "Soldier! Will you work? No, sirree—I'll sell my shirt first!"

For a man who would end up leading armies through the most dangerous and rugged of terrains, Grant was notoriously sensitive on a personal level. It is a bit unclear what exactly the gist of the mockery was; perhaps it was a reference to Grant's dress shirt. But whatever the context, the youth's uncouth remarks were enough to ruin this West Point graduate's day. This can be evidenced by the fact that the cruel words can still be quoted. Grant obviously remembered them for the rest of his life.

Grant wanted to be someone, and here this ruffian was trying to burst his bubble. Most would probably just shrug off the abuse for what it was—a jealous young man trying to get under a rival's skin. But Grant tended to take personal attacks very poorly. If openly ridiculed, Grant would be sent spiraling into a moment of introspection in which he would start to question himself.

Making matters worse, when he returned to Bethel, a local troublemaker became even more inventive in his ridicule of Grant by actually putting on a pair of blue pants that he had sewn a white stripe onto. The youth was determined to make a mockery of the recently graduated officer, and he began strutting down the street in what amounted to a mock march, all at the expense of Ulysses S. Grant.

Again, most of us, when provoked by a couple of local troublemakers like this, would probably ask ourselves, "Who are these people? And why would their opinion matter?" They were a couple of nobodies, so their mockery should have meant nothing. However, Grant took their actions hard, almost as if it were someone important declaring that he was no good. And the old taunts of his youth, in which folks said that "Ulysses was Useless," came to the forefront of his mind.

Instead of dismissing the taunts, Ulysses carried them with him. From that moment on, he would claim that such taunts provoked within him "a distaste for military uniform" that he "never recovered from." Interestingly enough, in his later career, Grant would be known to dumb down his uniform, making it as rugged and unpretentious as possible. Rather than strutting in a full officer's uniform, he was likely to wear the most average looking of uniforms, as it was the least likely to get attention.

It seems that it all stemmed from these isolated incidents that made such an impression on him after his graduation. He was mocked for "showing off," so he decided to keep his uniform as low-key as possible in the future. It is amazing how a couple of low-lives like this could influence a great man like Ulysses S. Grant, but this is apparently what happened.

Nevertheless, Grant showed up on time at the Jefferson Barracks in Missouri that fall, just as planned. This military installation was made up of a series of impressive stone structures, which were neatly encircled by a white picket fence. In his role with the 4th Infantry, Grant was part of a unit that consisted of roughly seven thousand troops. Grant would run into many former classmates from West Point here.

He even came across his old roommate from the academy—Frederick T. Dent. Grant would see Dent quite a bit during his stay at Jefferson Barracks. This was a particularly useful friendship since Dent's family was only a few miles away, giving Grant a good home away from home. This second home would also prove to be quite pivotal for his personal future since he ended up marrying one of Frederick Dent's sisters—the striking Julia.

Grant first met Julia in February of 1844 when she was eighteen. He had made it a habit to regularly visit the Dent household, and Julia was a major draw. Although later biographers would claim that Julia was not the most physically attractive woman, Grant seemed to be drawn to her lively personality more than anything else. Julia Dent was outgoing and humorous, and her talkative nature was just the thing that Grant needed to break through his own cold, standoffish exterior.

One other thing about Julia really appealed to the young Ulysses; she happened to know her way around a horse! As it turns out, she was an excellent horse rider. Grant and Julia frequently rode alongside one another, and the couple would quickly bond.

According to Julia, Grant was a daily visitor. The only trouble was his routine visits sometimes made him late for his engagements at the Jefferson Barracks. On one occasion, he was so hesitant to leave his love that he ended up late for dinner in the barrack's mess hall. In the highly regimented barracks, this was a big no-no.

Grant's superior officer—Captain Robert C. Buchanan—had an interesting means of punishing those who dared come down to the mess hall late. He required the tardy individual to purchase a bottle of wine for the entire mess hall to enjoy. As Grant and Julia's relationship advanced, Grant supposedly had to buy more than one bottle of wine before it was all said and done.

Little did Grant know that his whole world would soon abruptly change due to developments on the national stage. The drama centered around Texas. Texas had been part of Mexico, but it boasted a large number of American settlers. These settlers rebelled against Mexican authorities and fought a revolution to become an independent republic. Texas ultimately came out on top, and in the subsequent years, Texas would be a sovereign nation to itself. However, from the very beginning of Texas independence, there were

Americans both outside and inside Texas who wanted Texas to join the Union.

There were a couple of reasons why the US was hesitant to accept Texas. For one thing, they did not want to press their luck with Mexico. But even more controversial for the state of the Union was the fact that Texas had slaves. At the time, the United States was made up of "free states," which were primarily in the North, in which slavery was illegal, and "slave states," which were primarily in the South, in which slavery was still allowed.

Everyone knew that Texas would enter the Union as a slave state. The Northern states feared that it would give the Southern states more influence and an advantage over them. As such, many were hesitant to allow Texas to be admitted since doing so would disrupt the delicate balance of power between the free states and the slave states.

Nevertheless, the war drums started to beat, and as tensions between the US and Mexico flared, war was declared. Grant knew that he would be away for a while, so he sought some reassurance for his potential future with Julia. He actually tried to give her his class ring from West Point, informing her that he always wanted to hand the ring off to the woman he intended to marry.

Without directly saying it, Grant was basically proposing that the two start their engagement. But Julia, who was still young and not quite ready for such a big step, found herself taken aback. In a flustered manner, she entirely sidestepped the whole thing by declaring, "Oh no! Mama would never approve of my accepting a gift from a gentleman!"

Julia acted as if it was a simple matter of not wishing to take a gift, but in doing so, she refused to even consider the actual proposal that was being made. Grant, who was already sensitive about his prospects and keen to avoid rejection, was devastated. He was not ready to give up, though. A couple of weeks later, Grant finally came right out and asked the woman he loved if she would marry him. To which she is said to have replied, "It would be charming to be engaged, but married? No! I would rather be engaged."

The answer is a bit puzzling, but it was good enough for Grant. They would be engaged to be married. Julia only had one caveat: she told her newfound fiancé, "Don't tell Papa!" But this time around, Julia did indeed accept Grant's ring.

Chapter 3 – Headed Off to War

"The art of war is simple enough. Find out where your enemy is. Get at him as soon as you can. Strike him as hard as you can, and keep moving on."

-*Ulysses S. Grant*

After hostilities came to a breaking point with Mexico over America's decision to annex Texas, Ulysses S. Grant found himself headed off to war. In March of 1846, Ulysses S. Grant received his marching orders to head to Fort Texas near the Rio Grande River. The fort had been hastily built in anticipation of an attack by Mexican forces from the other side of the waterway.

The Mexican government, which considered the Nueces River as the rightful border with Texas at the time, considered the mobilization of military force on the Rio Grande as an act of war. Things then came to a head on April 25th, 1846, when the Mexican cavalry arrived on the scene. The men crossed the Rio Grande and launched an assault on some sixty-three dragoons. This attack killed eleven Americans and wounded several others. Those who survived the ordeal were taken as prisoners of war.

Washington had been looking for a reason for war with Mexico, and it had found it. This led to an all-out battle erupting on May 8th between a force of around 2,300 American troops and about 4,000 Mexican soldiers in Palo Alto (near modern-day Brownsville, Texas). The Mexican forces were led by the legendary Santa Anna, a great military strategist who was known as the "Napoleon of the West."

Santa Anna's larger force was indeed impressive, but their arms were hopelessly outdated compared to the weapons used by the Americans. Grant and his comrades were using powerful artillery, the best rapid-fire rifles, whereas the Mexican troops were stuck with outdated Spanish guns that were slow to load and slow to fire. Unable to withstand the withering gunfire arrayed against them and after losing some three hundred troops in a matter of minutes, the Mexican Army was forced to retreat. The US troops, in the meantime, had only lost five soldiers. Five for three hundred—it was a stunning victory for the Americans and a clear sign of what was to come.

In later years, Grant would come to regret the war, feeling that it was an unjust conflict that bullied the Mexicans out of their land. In the aftermath of the American Civil War in the 1860s, this was a fairly popular view among Republicans like Grant. The war with Mexico had come to be seen as a precursor of the Civil War in the sense that the Southerners' push to annex Texas as a "slave state" put America on a trajectory that would lead to civil strife.

But Grant's views toward the end of his life were likely much different than they were during the war. Although his thoughts at the time were not recorded, this young man must have been fairly enthusiastic since he was caught up in these incredible wars on the ground. At any rate, the Mexican Army regrouped after the Battle of Palo Alto in a place known as the Resaca de la Palma.

Here, the Mexican positions holed up behind a backdrop of thick vegetation and swamps, which denied the pursuing American troops direct access to the Mexicans. There would be no long-range potshots; instead, the terrain ensured that most of the fighting would be up close and personal. The Mexicans hoped that this would neutralize the Americans' technological advantage by forcing them to take part in what amounted to practically hand-to-hand combat with a much larger army.

Grant's unit was one of those that was led through the maze of these swamplands under fire from the Mexicans. At one point, Grant navigated through a couple of ponds and literally led the way, raising his saber and crying out, "Charge!" There would be countless charges into the waiting enemy, but the Americans finally prevailed.

Despite their larger numbers, the Mexican Army fell to pieces when faced with the relentless and tenacious Americans. Soon, the American forces had marched on the Mexican city of Matamoros, and they dug in their heels to occupy the town. By August, Grant had been promoted to the position of quartermaster of his 4th Infantry unit.

Grant was pleased with the pay increase, but he was not happy with the fact that this position took him away from the front lines. Grant wanted to be able to take charge and distinguish himself in battle; being the quartermaster decreased the odds of him being able to do so. Grant was so upset that he actually appealed the decision with a superior officer named Lieutenant Colonel John Garland, demanding that the army reconsider. Grant wrote, "I respectfully protest against being assigned to a duty which removes me from sharing in the dangers and honors of service with my company at the front."

Despite all of his appeals, there was no negotiation. Grant would be quartermaster, and that was that. Grant was picked for the role because of his leadership ability and meticulous attention to detail. The quartermaster was to make sure that the troops were in order and that supplies were at the ready. As part of his role, Grant was sent on scouting missions all over the recently occupied sections of Mexico. He was to be on the lookout for goods and resources that could be requisitioned for the US Army's efforts.

One of the most important goods that Grant requisitioned was a detailed map of Mexico, which he had purchased from a Mexican teamster. It is believed that this teamster had somehow stolen the map from a Mexican general. Due to decades of political instability, Mexico was in a state of constant upheaval, and there was always a black market of illicit goods and underground (possibly stolen) merchandise.

It is not entirely clear how this Mexican teamster got a hold of this map, but it was a top-notch piece of cartography, as it was detailed enough to be used by the Mexican military. It would prove to be a vital tool for the Americans as they pushed deeper into Mexican territory. Grant and company would soon drive some two hundred miles west of Matamoros and began to lay siege to the city of Monterrey.

The Mexican Army was in full force here, and after three days of fighting, there was a tremendous loss of life on both sides. Grant, who was staying true to the role of quartermaster, watched from a distance. That was his role, and those were his orders. But after the third day of seeing his fellow soldiers fight and die in this heated conflict, he could no longer bring himself to follow such a directive.

In one bold moment, he hopped onto his horse and charged right into the heat of the battle. He arrived just in time to find his own unit attempting to mount an attack on the Mexican artillery. Initially, the plan was to launch an assault on this Mexican artillery so that the firepower would be diverted toward the attacking unit, therefore giving cover to the main bulk of the army attempting to enter the city.

Things did not go quite so well, and the unit was repulsed with devastating losses, which included the death of the 4th Infantry's adjutant. Grant was immediately requisitioned to fill in the role of the slain commander. After a couple more days of bloody fighting, the Americans finally breached the city. However, they did not get too far since the Mexican troops, which were holed up in nearby residences, were hitting the Americans with a blistering barrage of fire if they dared to advance.

The Mexican Army appeared to be well stocked in supplies, which stood in stark contrast to the ill-equipped Americans. In fact, many of the troops were becoming dangerously low on ammunition. If the enemy realized how precarious their situation was, it was possible that a sudden massive counter-offensive on their part could have decimated the invading Americans. It was realized that someone needed to get the word out to Major General David Twiggs, who was positioned far from the battlefield, that more supplies were needed.

Grant readily volunteered to ride off to the distant base camp to make this request known. It has been said that Grant rode out of Monterrey while employing one of his favorite tricks in horse riding. With one foot hooked into the side saddle, he stood with his whole body on one side of the horse. He then purposefully rode away from the conflict with only his horse's body exposed to gunfire. This was perhaps smart for a soldier but certainly a bit disconcerting for the horse!

Nevertheless, despite several shots sent his way, both he and the horse were left unscathed. Once Grant was away from the danger of Monterrey, he then rode normally back to the base camp to let them know what was happening. But his trip proved to be futile. While he was gone, a seismic shift had occurred on the battlefield. Both sides were tired and beaten, and after the Americans pulled back, the two sides entered into negotiations with one another.

Although the Mexicans clearly had the upper hand at this stage, as one strong counter-offensive could have possibly defeated the American contingent, the Americans were able to persuade the Mexicans into thinking that their best option would be for both sides to agree to a truce.

As part of the agreement, the Mexican Army was allowed to peacefully depart with all of their weapons and supplies, while the Americans were left to occupy what was left of Monterrey. The American commanders were essentially playing a bluffing game with the Mexican Army. In reality, they knew that if the Mexican military were to unite as one and launch a major unified offensive against them, they would be driven out.

But the Mexican military, like much of Mexican society at the time, was hopelessly fractured. Rather than being able to present one unified force, there were several smaller factions that were either not willing or not able to work together. The forces at Monterrey were just one of these patchwork factions of the Mexican Army.

There were even occasions in which American troops were not exactly sure who they were fighting. Grant himself found this out shortly after the truce when he led a foraging expedition in northern Mexico to requisition some badly needed staple goods for the troops. During this foray, Grant's group was ambushed by a motley crew that seemed to consist of some Mexican troops as well as outright desperadoes and ordinary local townspeople.

Nevertheless, Grant and company fought hard. Although they were outnumbered, they won the day. Grant himself glowingly reported to one of his superior officers, "I lost one man and had a horse wounded. We captured three of the enemy, three horses and a flag, and we had a handsome fight!"

By 1847, however, US President James Polk was looking for a quick end to the conflict. It was then that the military high command determined that the best way to bring a quick and decisive end to the conflict was to take the battle to Mexico's capital—Mexico City. And the best way to march on Mexico City with a limited number of troops and supplies would be to land a force by sea near the shores of Veracruz.

It would be a straight drive to the Mexican capital from there. Grant was part of this invasion force, which landed at Veracruz on March 9th, 1847. Grant, along with his fellow comrades in arms, came to shore aboard so-called "surf boats," which were sent from the main naval craft. It was eerily quiet when they landed. Surprisingly enough, there was no Mexican Army there to greet them.

The main hardship these invaders faced was simply dealing with the elements. Even in March, it was a hot day, and many of the troops had the misery of dealing with sandstorms, with sand relentlessly pelting them in the face and obscuring their vision. Nevertheless, the Americans came ashore and soon wrapped around the port city of Veracruz.

Although they came ashore unopposed, taking the heavily fortified city of Veracruz would not be easy. The Americans made use of their long-range artillery, launching explosive rounds into Mexican positions that were well within the city limits. The Mexicans shot off a blistering array of bullets around the clock. The Americans dug in and did their best to dodge the bombs and bullets being hurled at them.

The siege ultimately lasted for three weeks before the defenders of Veracruz gave up and handed over the keys to their city to the Americans. After solidifying their position at Veracruz, the Americans then marched onward to the inland capital of Mexico—Mexico City. The Mexican Army, which was led by the legendary Santa Anna, rode out to meet the invaders and set up shop some fifty miles from Veracruz.

They dug into their position in the mountainous region, ready to ambush the Americans as soon as they came near. None other than Robert E. Lee would thwart these plans by finding a side route that would allow the Americans to go around the Mexican positions.

It is worth noting that during this conflict, Grant would get to know his later "arch-nemesis" in the American Civil War —Robert E. Lee— quite well. They were acquaintances, and some might even say friends by the time the Mexican-American War ran its course. And as many historians have pointed out, it was this close association from the past that helped smooth over Lee's ultimate surrender to Grant at the end of the American Civil War.

At any rate, this ingenious tactic of Lee's allowed the Americans to launch a surprise attack on the Mexicans who had been sent to surprise attack them! As American troops closed in from behind, the Mexican troops were shocked to suddenly sustain an assault from their back flanks.

In the meantime, Grant was busy making sure the supply lines were in order. Once the fight commenced, he tried to catch up, but he was not able to regroup with the main contingent. Instead, he positioned himself with an artillery battery fielded by Lieutenant George McClellan. From here, all Grant could do was watch the main battle as it unfolded in the distance.

After the Mexican troops began to retreat, Grant and McClellan both decided to charge forward and fight alongside the rest of the Americans. The battle was all but over by the time they arrived on the scene. The army then marched on Mexico City as planned, reaching the gates of this Mexican metropolis that September.

The general in charge of it all, Winfield Scott, was soon making his headquarters inside the famed Hall of Montezuma. This was a feat that helped give rise to the military anthem known as the "Marines' Hymn," which proudly proclaims, "From the Halls of Montezuma/To the shores of Tripoli!"

As for Ulysses S. Grant? For all of his efforts, he was given the rank of first lieutenant. Not bad for a soldier still in his twenties. Mexico ended up suing for peace and signed the Treaty of Guadalupe Hidalgo on February 2nd, 1848. This treaty ceded all land north of the Rio Grande to the United States in exchange for the US paying $15 million in damages and taking on about $3.5 million of Mexico's debts in the region.

Grant was most likely relieved that the war was over. Still, American soldiers were not able to make their way home until that summer. It was already June when Grant made his way to Veracruz, where he and the other soldiers were to disembark for repatriation back to the US.

However, Ulysses S. Grant ran into some mischief along the way when he misplaced a large amount of money. As quartermaster, it was his responsibility to safeguard the quartermaster funds, and he was carrying a sum of about $1,000 in a locked trunk as he journeyed to Veracruz. As Lieutenant DeRussy of the 4th Infantry would later recall about the night of June 16th, 1848, "the trunk containing said funds was stolen from the tent of Capt. Gore, this whilst Capt. Gore and myself were both sleeping in the tent."

No one seemed to know what had happened to the money, but since it was Grant who was in charge of carrying the funds, he was ultimately held responsible. The bill he owed would be a lingering, unpleasant reminder of the war. Nevertheless, Grant made his way to Veracruz and boarded a boat with several other soldiers. They set sail for Pascagoula, Mississippi, arriving on American soil that July.

After acquiring a two-month leave, Grant then made his way back to the arms of his beloved Julia Dent. The two were wed on August 22nd, 1848, in St. Louis, Missouri. Grant knew that wars were lost and wars were won, but as it pertained to him personally, his marriage to his wife was the greatest victory he had ever achieved.

Chapter 4 – Grant's Lonely Outpost

"The friend in my adversity I shall always cherish most. I can better trust those who helped to relieve the gloom of my dark hours than those who are so ready to enjoy with me the sunshine of my prosperity."

-Ulysses S. Grant

Soon after their wedding, Grant received new marching orders. He was to man a post in Detroit. His newly married bride, Julia, was not exactly thrilled with the prospect. She broke down in tears at the thought of leaving the comfortable laidback lifestyle she had with her parents. Her father had a solution: Julia could stay with them, and Grant could simply visit her on leave.

This, of course, would have been a highly abnormal relationship. A military man like Grant should not be forced to go to his post by himself and then travel a great distance while on leave just to see his wife! Grant was frustrated by the suggestion. He asked his wife, "Would you like to remain with your father and let me go alone?" Fortunately for Grant, Julia choked back her tears and agreed to go with him.

The couple left for Grant's new posting as the regimental quartermaster of Fort Detroit in November of 1848. He arrived just in time to receive what appeared to be a puzzling change of plans. He was told that he had been reassigned to Sackets Harbor, New York. Apparently, the quartermaster who had filled in for Grant refused to leave his post. This quartermaster made it clear that he was not about to uproot himself in the middle of winter.

Due to this, Grant and his wife had to abruptly leave Detroit and head to the post at Sackets Harbor, where they would spend a freezing winter in the full chill that only Lake Ontario can provide. One can only imagine the distress of Julia, who had given up her happy, comfortable life with her parents for this hardship.

In the meantime, Grant lodged a formal complaint with the War Department. By the spring of 1849, it was agreed to send him down to Detroit. Here, the arrangements were a little more conducive for the young couple, and they were able to set up shop in a permanent home of their own. It was a small house in a lower-income section of Detroit, but for the Grants, it was a good enough start. And Grant's job was secure.

It was so secure, in fact, that he found out that there was very little for him to do. He was the quartermaster of a quiet military outpost during peacetime. Most of his job consisted of occasional filling out papers and overseeing the routine drills of soldiers under his charge. But much of his tenure involved a whole lot of nothing, coupled with a constant vigilance just in case something should happen.

There is an old motto in the army: it is a valuable skill to learn how one can "hurry up and wait." Although the expression itself was likely developed after Grant's time (some believe it was coined during World War Two), Grant most certainly learned the gist of it. And he learned it quite well. In many ways, his role at Fort Detroit was a glorified desk job—something which Grant detested. As he would later remark, "I was no clerk, nor had I any capacity to become one."

In the midst of all this boredom, Grant's wife Julia discovered that she was pregnant. This was a joyous occasion, but since Julia decided to finally take her parents up on their offer of room and board—at least for the pregnancy—Grant was left disappointed once again. Julia would later claim that a doctor had specifically told her to go home to St. Louis so that there would not be any complications. But historians have long doubted that she ever received such a recommendation. All the same, Julia no doubt benefited from having her parents and other family members near her to help her through her pregnancy.

At any rate, with the departure of his wife, Ulysses S. Grant was left to fend for himself once again. She would be separated from her husband for about eight months before giving birth to their first child—Frederick Dent Grant—in May of 1850. Grant then obtained a much-needed leave from Detroit and headed off to St. Louis to reunite with his wife and meet his firstborn son.

The young family of three headed back to Detroit that October. It was another cold winter in Detroit, and as it progressed, Grant found himself in an interesting legal spectacle. One day, Grant walked in front of the home of a successful, local businessman by the name of Zachariah Chandler. Chandler had apparently neglected to clear the ice and snow from the sidewalk in front of his home.

Grant stepped on a patch of ice, lost his footing, and fell down. Grant was so incensed by the mishap that he filed a lawsuit against Chandler, suing for injuries sustained from the fall. The official lawsuit described the suit as being due to Chandler failing "to keep his sidewalk free and clear from snow and ice." This case went to trial, and Grant actually won.

But it seems the jury was upset over the pettiness of the lawsuit, so they made sure that the damages awarded to Grant were equally petty. In the end, Chandler was ordered to pay six cents to Grant—which was a minuscule amount of money even back in the 1800s! Grant was also forced to be subjected to public ridicule during the course of the proceedings, with Chandler basically accusing him of being a drunk.

At one point, Chandler railed, "If you soldiers would keep sober—perhaps you would not fall on people's pavements and hurt your legs!"

It is unclear if Grant was drunk at the time, but in truth, he had picked up a regular drinking habit that would follow him for the rest of his life. It is believed that he had developed a soft spot for liquor during his days in the Mexican-American War, and he was frequently seen with booze thereafter.

Interestingly enough, Chandler would later become a senator, and he actually managed to become a part of the future President Grant's cabinet as the secretary of the interior. Both men showed that they could let bygones be bygones. Apparently, they both laughed about the incident later in life and viewed each other good-naturedly from there on out.

As it pertains to the winter of 1850, however, Grant was not too pleased with either the verdict of the Detroit jury or his superior officers. Soon after this, he learned that he would have to pack once again, as he would be headed back to Sackets Harbor, New York. Julia, for one, made it clear that if Grant went, she was not going to join him. She cited the unbearable cold as her reason to stay behind. She and her young son left Grant to stay with her parents, forcing the disillusioned husband and father to head off to his lonely outpost in Sackets Harbor by himself.

Grant would write to his wife frequently to see how things were going, mainly to check on his son, who he often referred to offhandedly as "the little dog." But as much as Grant wanted to keep in touch with what was happening with his wife and child, her perceived lack of interest in readily replying left him depressed and frustrated.

At one point, she went several weeks without saying a word, prompting Grant to snap. "After a lapse of more than one month—I at length received a letter from you yesterday. I do not see that you had any excuse whatever for not writing before." He then sternly warned her, "Do not neglect to write for so long a time again." But no matter how much Grant voiced his frustrations with his wife, she not only tended to take them in stride but also ignored them. Her correspondence to him would remain infrequent.

Grant, in the meantime, passed the summer months of 1851 by making trips to outlying regions when he could. At one point, he even took an excursion to Montreal.

By the following fall, he finally managed to get his wife and child to join him in Sackets Harbor. The reunion was pleasant enough, but it was brief. By the time winter had arrived, Julia had discovered that she was pregnant once again. This gave her all the excuse she needed, and she was soon off to St. Louis once again. It was in the cold and lonely isolation of Sackets Harbor that Grant's drinking took a turn for the worse.

In fact, his drinking habit had become bad enough that he sought an intervention. Fortunately for him, there was help to be found. He joined a local lodge called the Sons of Temperance. He showed up at weekly meetings held in the local Presbyterian church. The group not only helped him to control his drinking habit but also provided a much-needed social outlet for Grant. Grant was soon a full-fledged member of the lodge, and he participated in all of the lodge's events.

Although Grant's penchant for alcohol would come back to haunt him later, at this point in his life, he was happy to put it to the side. At any rate, Grant managed to get through that dark winter.

In the spring of 1852, Grant was given new marching orders. He was told that he would be headed for a military outpost in California. Upon hearing this news, Julia actually offered to head off with her husband for a change. But Grant thought that the trip would be too bothersome for a woman who was about to give birth, so he actually told her to stay behind.

It was indeed a long, complicated trip. It was not just an excursion overland. It involved Grant getting on a boat in New York Harbor and then sailing all the way to the thin strip of land between South America and North America known as the Panama isthmus. This isthmus was then crossed on land to the Pacific. There, Grant got on another ship and sailed right up to the California coast. Making use of the isthmus as a shortcut to the Pacific Ocean was perhaps quicker than a straight shot overland, but it certainly did not make the trip any less arduous or dangerous since both accidents and sickness at sea were quite common.

It seems that soon after setting sail, Grant put aside his previous decision to abstain from alcohol, as he was quite frequently seen with a bottle in his hand. The booze no doubt helped him ease both the boredom and rigors of the trip. Grant also drank alcohol simply to avoid drinking cholera-infected water. There had been several outbreaks among passengers at the time. It is possible that Grant sought to avoid sickness by simply partaking of wine rather than water.

Upon reaching Panama, Grant and company trekked overland the remaining thirty-five miles to the other side of the isthmus so that they could hop on a ship to take them to the Pacific coast of California. This was before the creation of the Panama Canal, of course, so this overland excursion was the only way Panama could be crossed. The overland trek, though short, was a hard one due to the rugged terrain, tropical heat, and the frequent outbreak of disease.

Considering all of this, Grant was most likely correct in his assumption that his wife would be best left at home. The journey was dangerous enough for a man in full, perfect health, so it certainly would not have been easy for someone like Julia, who was heavily pregnant at the time. Nevertheless, Grant and his fellow soldiers made their way to the other side of the Panama isthmus on July 26th, 1852.

By then, several of the men who had accompanied him had perished along the way. Most of them had succumbed to the aforementioned cholera outbreak. It is indeed amazing what Grant and his peers had to go through simply to cross one side of America to the other. The incident would stick with Grant. Upon becoming president, he urged Congress of the need to create "a path between the seas." It was musings like this that would eventually lead to the construction of the Panama Canal, which would allow ships to pass from one side of the continent to the other without their passengers having to disembark on a dangerous overland route.

Nevertheless, Grant was able to board the ship waiting to take him to California—the Golden Gate. This freighter took him and his fellow survivors from the west coast of Panama to the west coast of California, arriving in August of 1852.

Grant landed in San Francisco, which at that time was comprised of around fifty thousand people. The city was small by today's standards, but it was still a wild metropolis in its own right back then—and that fifty thousand had arrived at a rapid rate. Many souls came during the 1848 Gold Rush, which created a hectic mix of hopeful newcomers ready to strike it rich.

Ulysses S. Grant ended up settling in at a town called Benicia, which was some fifteen miles north of San Francisco. There, he took some time to recover from the rigors of his previous journey. Grant's wife Julia had given birth to their second son in the meantime and named him after their father, christening the child Ulysses Jr.

Grant desperately yearned for his family to join him, but a reunion was not yet in the cards. Instead, once he felt better, he hopped on a steamboat and sailed up to Fort Vancouver, which was located some eight miles north of Portland, Oregon. Grant had a lot of downtime there, and he proceeded to use it to pursue various schemes to make money. His first enterprise was to partner with a merchant by the name of Elijah Camp to set up a general store in the vicinity of Fort Vancouver. The store was a success, but Elijah Camp managed to convince Grant into selling his share of the business. Grant was able to make $1,500 by doing so.

However, Grant would soon regret his decision, as he later realized that if he had kept his co-ownership of the store, he could have made as much as $3,000 every year. Nevertheless, Grant moved on to his next money-making scheme. He wanted to get into the potato market since he realized that one could make $8 a bushel for this in-demand bit of produce.

In order to make this enterprise happen, he hooked up with a local farmer by the name of Ogden. He let Grant use his land for farming if Grant worked on the fencing on the property. It was certainly enough to keep him busy. Ogden's property was sprawling, and on top of that, Grant had to tend to his budding potatoes on the farm. He was successful in growing a massive crop of potatoes, but unfortunately for him, the demand for them dropped just as soon as he was ready to sell them.

By the time harvest time came around, it seemed as if just about everyone in the San Francisco Bay area had the same idea as him. The market was absolutely flooded with potatoes. This massive supply brought down demand, and it, in turn, sunk the price from eight dollars a bushel to approximately twenty-five cents. In the end, Grant did not even make enough money to cover the expenses racked up from tending the farm.

This business failure was followed by another when he attempted to start selling logs, which was then followed by a failed pig farm. Soon after that, Grant went into the hotel business, leasing space with some fellow officers in the San Francisco area. This was the one enterprise that seemed to be successful—that is, until the manager put on Grant's payroll suddenly decided to skip town with all of the money that had been made.

It seemed that whatever Grant tried to invest his time, money, and effort into was an abject failure. In the midst of this misery, Grant was again transferred, this time to Fort Humboldt in the northern reaches of California. That fall, he was promoted to captain. It should have been a happy moment, but all Grant felt was despair.

He was over a thousand miles from his wife, who was raising children who he barely knew. All he wanted to do was get back to them. Grant just could not take the separation any longer, and so, at thirty-two years of age when most had firmly settled into their military careers, Grant made the fateful decision to give it all up and resign.

Chapter 5 – Living a Hardscrabble Life

"My failures have been errors in judgment, not of intent."
  -*Ulysses S. Grant*

After submitting his resignation, Grant borrowed some money from his friend and fellow West Point alum Simon Bolivar Buckner (who would fight in the Civil War on the Confederate side) and headed off to reunite with his family in St. Louis. Grant went back the same way he had; it was not an easy journey. He sailed to Panama and once again crossed the Panama isthmus before sailing to New York. After an exhausted and nearly broke Ulysses S. Grant reached a hotel in New York, he contacted both his wife and his parents to let them know of his whereabouts.

Jesse's father back in Ohio was absolutely appalled when he heard of what his son had done. Upon learning of his son's resignation, he immediately sent out a letter to the secretary of war—Jefferson Davis—to ask for his son's reinstatement. Yes, the future president of the Confederacy, Jefferson Davis, was the same man who was the secretary of war when Grant tendered his resignation.

Jesse pleaded with Davis, explaining that his son had made a rash decision under the duress of being separated from his family. He asked Davis to give him a six-month furlough instead so that he could go back to his post afterward. Davis was no help, stating that it was too late, and refused to intercede on Ulysses's behalf.

Grant made his way from New York to his parents' homestead in Covington. After a distressing reunion with his worried parents, he then made his way to St. Louis, Missouri, to see his wife and kids. It has been said that when Ulysses pulled up at the Dent family homestead, his two sons were playing out front and ran away when their father approached. To them, he was just a stranger.

After this strange reunion with his wife and children, Grant and his family were allowed to stay at a house that Julia's brother Louis had constructed on the family property. However, Grant did not like living under someone else's roof, so he decided to literally build his own roof.

In the spring of 1855, he built a simple, modest house that he and his family would call home, at least for a time. He cut down trees, fashioned the wood, built doors and the chimney, and installed the windows. It was not easy, and he named the place appropriately, calling it his "hardscrabble" estate.

Grant, who had financial help from his father Jesse, then began to start his own farm on the homestead. Along with raising crops, he also sold firewood to make extra money. Another source of revenue was through renting out his horse. It was indeed a hardscrabble existence, but two things made Grant happy, even in the midst of his hardship—being near his family and being able to keep busy.

Previously, Grant had been drowning in despair, sitting at a military barracks, lonely and with nothing to do. Now, he had enough on his plate to keep him occupied all day long, and at the end of the day, he had a wife and kids to come home to. And his family was growing. His wife Julia gave birth to his third child, a daughter named Ellen, on July 4th, 1855. Grant was overjoyed to be a father again.

Even so, life on the farm would soon prove to be too much for Grant. He worked his fingers to the bone, and he developed bad arthritis as a result. Making matters worse, he had recurring bouts of malaria symptoms, an illness he first came down with on his way back from California. Julia was not liking life at "Hardscrabble" either. And just a few months into this experiment, she found an excuse to extricate the family from the homestead.

Her mother passed away, and she was able to make the case that she and Grant should move the family back into her dad's house under the guise of looking after him. So, that was what they did. Grant managed to rent out the Hardscrabble house to someone, and they headed off to Mr. Dent's estate. The experience would prove to be quite miserable for Grant.

His father-in-law, the "southern gentleman," had always viewed his "Yankee" son-in-law with a certain degree of contempt even before he quit the army. And now that he was perceived as a drop-out with dismal financial prospects, Dent looked down on Grant all the more. His previous disdain, which had been carefully masked, was now out in the open.

In the fall of 1857, the US entered a bad economic recession. Life for almost everyone became just a little more difficult and frustrating. By the time the holiday season arrived, Grant found himself unable to buy even the cheapest of Christmas gifts. In order to raise some cash, he was forced to sell his gold watch. Complicating matters even further, by the following spring, Grant had another mouth to feed. His youngest child, Jesse, was born on February 6th, 1858. The baby was named in honor of Grant's father.

The family would struggle on. The situation would not improve much in the next couple of years, and by the spring of 1860, Grant finally accepted his own father's offers of help. Jesse had been trying to get Grant to move up to Galena, Illinois, to work in his prospering leather business. With no other prospects in life, Grant finally answered the call. He rented out a modest, seven-room home for his family and set to work to become his father's apprentice.

It was quite a turnaround for Grant. As a young man, he had sworn to his father that he would not go into business with him. But now, as he approached middle age, he was attempting to do just that. He was essentially a low-level clerk. Even more humiliating, he was under the supervision of his younger brothers—Simpson and Orvil. The scrutiny was high, the pay was mediocre, and the work was boring. Everyone knew that Grant's heart was not in it. But he had no choice.

In the meantime, the nation as a whole was becoming increasingly tense over the issue of slavery. The Southern states supported the Democratic Party, which in those days was supportive of slavery, whereas the North was becoming increasingly supportive of the Republican Party, which advocated for ending the practice or at least placing more limitations on it. By the time of the election of 1860, the Republicans had nominated Abraham Lincoln, a critic of slavery, while the Democrats ended up with two candidates—Stephen A. Douglas and John C. Breckinridge. Democrat candidate Breckinridge was an outright supporter of slavery, while Stephen A. Douglas was viewed as a more moderate Democrat.

The political situation was a primary topic of conversation in Jesse's leather shop. As Grant packaged leather goods for customers, he was more often than not likely to hear some of the latest talk on the upcoming election. Grant himself was unable to vote since he had not been in the state of Illinois long enough to meet the residency requirement.

Nevertheless, even if he did not actually cast a ballot, he supported the moderate Democrat Stephen Douglas, although he admired Lincoln. Part of his reasoning for sticking with the Democratic Party was due to the fact that his wife's family was staunchly Democrat. Grant also knew that if Lincoln, an anti-slavery Republican, was elected, the slave-holding Democrats of the South would be so infuriated that they just might rebel.

Grant knew that this threat was real, as the tensions had been simmering for some time. From his experience back in St. Louis, he had heard open talk of such things firsthand. As Grant would reflect many years later, "It made my blood run cold to hear friends of mine, southern men, discuss dissolution of the Union as though it were a tariff bill."

It was indeed terrible to contemplate how easily chaos might erupt, but Grant was right. And before Abraham Lincoln was even sworn in, Grant's fear became a reality. The states of the South—starting with South Carolina—began to secede from the Union one by one. These states would join forces and become the Confederate States of America (CSA). They appointed former Secretary of War Jefferson Davis as their president.

The rightful president of the United States, Abraham Lincoln, was sworn in that March. He had quite a bit on his plate, to say the least. Lincoln wished to avoid war if it were possible, so he avoided direct military action in the first month of his administration. It was only when Confederate troops attacked a federally run fort in South Carolina—Fort Sumter—on April 12th, 1861, that President Lincoln knew that bloodshed was unavoidable. The Civil War had begun.

Chapter 6 – The Civil War Begins

"Everyone has his superstitions. One of mine has always been when I started to go anywhere, or to do anything, never to turn back or to stop until the thing intended was accomplished."

-*Ulysses S. Grant*

On April 16th, 1861, Ulysses S. Grant was seated at a town meeting at the local courthouse in Galena. The townspeople, just like practically everyone else in the nation, were on edge. They were frantic for news of what was happening and struggling to figure out what action they—if any—should take in the face of this oncoming storm.

The mayor of Galena was actually a Democrat, and although he was shocked at what was happening, he at first attempted to sympathize with his fellow Democrat Southern secessionists. He agreed that leaving the Union was wrong under any circumstances, but he pleaded that brother shouldn't fight brother. He openly pleaded for a way to push back the tides of war.

The Republican congressman of the district was there as well, and predictably enough, he called everyone to arms to protect the Union and stop the secessionists. It was a twenty-nine-year-old local attorney named John A. Rawlins, however, who really stole the show. Grant knew Rawlings because he had worked for his father in the past.

Rawlings was a life-long Democrat, but the idea that states would actually leave the Union infuriated him. He spoke about his opinions to the crowd that gathered in that courthouse that day. He proclaimed, "I have been a Democrat all my life. But this is no longer a question of politics. It is simply union or disunion, country or no country. I have favored every honorable compromise, but the day for compromise is past. Only one course is left for us. We will stand by the flag of our country and appeal to the god of battles to vindicate our flag!"

It remains unclear exactly what "god of battles" the man might have been referring to, but the folks at the courthouse got the point. Soon, they were shouting and providing a lively chorus to his call for war. And although Grant may not have been quite as vociferous in his expression of it, he was among them. At that moment, Grant came to accept that a war to save the Union must be fought.

President Lincoln issued an order for seventy-five thousand able-bodied men to sign up for service in their local militias for a term that would supposedly last just a few months. This surge of volunteers was needed to compensate the official US Army, which at that time consisted of only around seventeen thousand troops. The troops of the Union were finite, and even the seventeen thousand who made up the official army were scattered across the nation.

For example, many had been sent west to man lonely outposts in the newly gained lands on the Pacific coast. It would take some time before they could regroup to face the threat of the Confederate Army, which was primarily centered in the southeast of the country. It was for this reason that volunteers from state-run militias were so crucial in defending the Union.

Although Grant had resigned from the military, he now had the perfect opportunity to put on a fighting uniform once again. Ulysses S.

Grant's newly adopted state of Illinois was asking for a total of six volunteer regiments. This led to the town of Galena rushing to hold a session in which to recruit men. Local Congressman Elihu B. Washburne, who knew of Grant's prior experience, saw to it that Grant presided over the discussion.

It was made known among the group that they wished for Grant to become the captain of the local militia, but he declined the responsibility. He still held out hope that he might somehow be able to return to the regular army. Nevertheless, he agreed to train and serve as a recruiter for the local militia.

On April 25th, Galena saw its very first unit of militia members assemble together in their dark blue and grey uniforms. These men were sent to the train depot, where they disembarked for Springfield. This was where the other local militias had gathered. One Ulysses S. Grant was among them. Grant had attempted to lobby the military to be reenlisted in the regular army, but his reinstatement was rejected.

However, with the support of Congressman Elihu B. Washburne, on April 29th, he was given the role of military aide to Illinois Governor Richard Yates. This meant a return to the boring deskwork that Grant loathed, as he had to fill out forms and keep track of inventory. But at $2 a day, he was simply glad it paid him well enough to get by.

Still, Grant held out hope that he could somehow be reinstated back into the regular army as an officer. Little did Grant know that Governor Yates was already hearing plenty of negative remarks about Grant from others. He was mercilessly referred to as a quitter and a deadbeat. The instance during the Mexican-American War in which he somehow let $1,500 get away from him as quartermaster was frequently mentioned as a reason to avoid Grant's reinstatement.

However, Grant would not give up. On May 24th, he went right over the governor of Illinois's head by writing a letter directly to the adjutant general in DC. He wrote the man, pleading to be given charge of one of the recently cobbled together infantry units on account of his previous experience.

In the letter, he wrote, "I would say that in view of my present age, and length of service, I feel myself competent to command a regiment." He was direct and to the point. It was indeed a simple enough request, but it would be left unanswered. Disillusioned, Grant drifted aimlessly for the next couple of months, seeking purpose. His luck was about to change when one of Illinois's regiments proved to be so disorderly and unruly that it needed a truly gifted hand at the helm.

It was then that Governor Yates began to reconsider Grant. And to Grant's great joy, on June 15th, he was informed that he had been selected to head the disorderly 21st Illinois Regiment, not as a volunteer captain but as an official colonel of the US Army. Grant would get his reinstatement after all.

Grant jumped at the chance. And although others would have been hesitant to command such a drunken, loudmouth bunch as the 21st Regiment was at the time, Grant had no fear. Just like the crazed and wild horses he had tamed in his youth, he was confident that he would eventually gain mastery over this unruly bunch as well. He believed they would soon fall in line under his calm, steady gaze. It would not be easy, but he would figure it out as he went along.

His crew was indeed a motley one. They did not even have uniforms. Most were in their work clothes, as they had come straight from the farm or the factory. Grant himself had no uniform save the beaten and battered rags he had saved from before his resignation from the military several years prior.

Nevertheless, Grant was ready to whip these men into shape. His quiet demeanor belied a real ruthlessness when he was in charge. Grant immediately made it clear that he would not tolerate any insubordination. Anyone who disagreed would be tied to a post until they decided to behave. He even had some of these men gagged in order to teach them from using profanity in his presence.

Grant was a real taskmaster, and it was amazing how he worked these men. And he soon had them falling in line. The regiment was officially sworn in on June 28th and then sent marching off to Quincy, Illinois. And when we say marching, we literally mean *marching*. Grant led the men directly on the ground as they made their way across the expanse of Illinois, traveling at a pace of about one hundred miles a week.

Grant knew from experience that such a task was good for the morale of the troops because it forced them to work together under hardship. The men learned how to walk with their heavy equipment and guns without missing a beat. Short of actually fighting in a battle, going on a long march overland was great for building up much-needed solidarity and discipline.

Grant was beaming with pride over his troops once they made it to Quincy. After looking his men over, he even went as far as to proclaim that they behaved as if they were "veteran troops in point of soldierly bearing, general good order, and cheerful execution of commands." Although these new recruits did well enough, equating them to "veteran troops" was perhaps laying it on a little thick.

Nevertheless, Grant wanted his men to know that he approved of their efforts. After their short stay in Quincy, Grant had his men march across the Illinois border with Missouri. In the northeast corner of Missouri, his regiment had its first assignment. They were to sniff out any potential Confederate guerrillas who might be lurking about and sabotaging bridges and rail lines.

Such things were indeed common enough during the war, so the idea of finding Confederates or Confederate sympathizers damaging federal property was not a far-fetched prospect. Things became serious when the group reached Palmyra, Missouri. Grant received orders to send them in pursuit of a large group of Rebels (another name for the Confederates) that were being commanded by Confederate General Thomas A. Harris.

Just before the first great challenge of the regiment, Grant began to have serious doubts. He was not fearful of his own life but rather the lives of those under his charge. He was now the leader of men, and he most certainly did not want to lead them all to early graves. The responsibility he had was beginning to weigh quite heavily on him. Nevertheless, he took a breath and prepared himself to lead his troops into battle.

But in this instance, the battle never arrived. They ended up finding General Harris's camp, but it was already deserted. Harris and company had apparently been tipped off that Grant and his men were coming, and they had decided to take off. Grant concluded that despite his misgivings, the Confederate troublemakers were apparently much more afraid of his advance than he was of confronting them. As Grant would later put it, "It occurred to me at once that Harris was much more afraid of me as I had been of him. This was a view of the question that I had never taken before; but it was one I never forgot afterwards."

The larger war was heating up, though. On July 21st, 1861, the Union Army suffered a terrible defeat at the Battle of Bull Run. The battle was just a short distance from the capital, and if the Confederates had pressed on, they might have threatened the White House. However, the Union Army ended up holding its ground, and the crisis was temporarily averted.

In the meantime, Grant received a promotion, reaching the rank of brigadier general on August 5th. In stark contrast to his days wasting away at lonely, remote military outposts, Grant was now right in the thick of things. Finally, his hard work was being recognized.

Grant and company were given new marching orders on August 7th. Grant was informed that his men were to head to his old stomping grounds of Jefferson Barracks. Plans abruptly changed, as they tend to do during wars, and Grant and his unit were sent off to Ironton, Missouri, instead.

This area was important for its industrial capacity, and it had reportedly been in danger of an attack by a group of Confederates. Grant immediately rushed his men over there, managing to cover some 110 miles in less than 24 hours' time. Upon his arrival, Grant was handed over a bit of intelligence, which stated that a large contingent of Rebel forces was getting ready to congregate in the low hills in the vicinity of Ironton.

Knowledge of being potentially outnumbered by a larger group of fighters could be a source of intimidation for anyone, but Grant kept his head. He plumbed the depths of his brain for a solid strategy, and he realized that success would require a good cavalry. This way, he could have men ready to mount their horses and scour the area for any interlopers headed their way.

He also knew that he needed to have some heavy artillery in place just in case a major standoff took place. Although the potential for trepidation was there, Grant told himself that the Confederate forces were no better trained or equipped than his and that they were likely just as fearful. If push did come to shove, Grant was confident that his unit could stand its ground.

Chapter 7 – Ready for Anything

"I appreciate the fact, and am proud of it, that the attentions I am receiving are intended more for our country than for me personally."

-Ulysses S. Grant

Grant and his men were ready for war in Ironton, but that is not what they got. After getting in place and preparing to be attacked, they learned that the Confederate forces had decided to take off. It was still early in the war for sure, but at this point, Grant must have lost any respect he might have had for the courage of the Confederates. To him, they seemed like a bunch of thugs launching hit-and-run attacks.

As soon as Grant heard that the Confederates were on the run, he made a conscious decision not to let them go. He wanted to send his troops in pursuit of them. It was not meant to be since the high command had other plans.

Grant's plans of pursuit were halted by none other than Brigadier General Benjamin M. Prentiss, a major player in the Battle of Shiloh. The brigadier general suddenly appeared at Grant's base camp and informed him that he had been reassigned by Major General John C. Fremont to southeastern Missouri.

Grant obviously did not like this decision, and he also felt he had a valid point of protest against it. Ulysses S. Grant knew that he outranked Prentiss because, although they were both brigadier generals for the militia, he was a captain in the regular army. This meant that he had seniority and that he trumped Prentiss. This, therefore, gave him a valid legal argument as it pertains to military protocol to argue against this decision. He sent his appeal to the War Department before heading off to Major General John Fremont's headquarters to report to him in person.

Grant presented his argument to Fremont in person, but Fremont did not agree. Fremont ended up ordering Grant to head over to a post in Jefferson City. Grant did not like this and asked to head back to Galena instead. This request was refused, so Grant was sent off to Jefferson City just as Fremont had intended.

But it would be a short stay. Just one week after his arrival, the War Department heard Grant's case and agreed with his argument that he had seniority over Prentiss. This indicated that there was a violation of military protocol, just as Grant had claimed. Fremont tried to make up for this slight by sending Grant to Cairo, Illinois. This city, which is located in southern Illinois, was a strategic stronghold. It put Grant in control of southern Illinois, as well as southeastern Missouri. Upon his arrival, Grant set up shop in an old bank building near the intersection of the Ohio and Mississippi Rivers.

At his new command post, Grant received some intelligence that the Confederates were going to march on Paducah, Kentucky. At that time, Kentucky was neutral, and the Union wanted to keep it that way. In order to prevent a Confederate takeover, something had to be done. Grant immediately rallied his troops and prepared to converge on Paducah, sending Fremont a telegram, stating simply, "I am getting ready to go to Paducah. Will start at 6 ½ o'clock."

As the evening wore on, Grant was still waiting for a response from Fremont. Grant eventually lost his patience waiting for Fremont's approval. He proclaimed to a military aide of his, "Come on. I can wait no longer. I will go if it costs me my commission." And Grant meant what he said; he had four artillery pieces put on three separate steamboats, along with a group of some 1,500 men under his command.

Grant's steamboats reached Paducah around eight in the morning, and he was able to take the town with ease. Although the Union was essentially an occupying force in a neutral Kentucky town, Grant presented himself and his comrades as liberators. He stood before all who would hear and proclaimed, "I have come among you, not as an enemy but as your friend and fellow citizen, not to injure or annoy you, but to defend and enforce the rights of all loyal citizens. I am here to defend you. I have nothing to do with opinions. I shall deal only with armed rebellion. The strong arm of the government is here to protect its friends, and to punish only its enemies."

Grant then left Brigadier General C. F. Smith in charge of the town and headed back up to Cairo, Illinois. Ironically enough, Grant finally received Fremont's response upon his return. Fremont instructed him to go ahead and proceed to Paducah "if you feel strong enough." Grant was glad that he had seized the moment when he could rather than waiting around for Fremont's weak-willed and delayed response.

Grant would become a much more decisive commander on the field after this venture. He relied more on his own instincts to make last-minute decisions, whether his superior officers agreed to it or not.

Fremont, in the meantime, managed to upset his own superior officer—President Abraham Lincoln. He did so by taking a heavy hand against the citizens of Paducah. Even though Grant had just proclaimed that the Union was their liberator and protector, Fremont took a draconian stance and sought to seize the lands of perceived Confederate sympathizers.

President Lincoln did not wish to alienate the populations of neutral states like Kentucky, so he told Fremont to take back his stringent measures. Fremont refused, and as a result, he was stripped of his authority. Grant was now under the direct oversight of Major General Henry W. Halleck instead. Halleck wanted to take a cautious but proactive approach. That November, he had Grant take his men and march them up and down the Mississippi River in an obvious show of force to deter the Confederates.

Grant did not want to simply deter the enemy; he was ready to take the fight to them. And so when he saw his opportunity, he struck. He led about three thousand troops to the town of Belmont, where a Confederate force had set up an encampment. Grant and his men were able to drive the Confederates out, but as soon as the surprise of the attack wore off, the Confederates were able to regroup.

They struck back at Grant and company. They had a larger force, and it became clear that Grant would have to lead his troops in a tactical retreat. He and his men were able to quickly board the steamboats and race back up the river with minimal losses.

Halleck was not exactly pleased with Grant's modification of his orders, but Grant described the operation as a successful raid and minimized the risk enough that Halleck ultimately decided to let it go. And after giving it some thought, Halleck decided to unleash Grant on a new target—Fort Henry in Tennessee.

This Confederate fort situated on the Cumberland River had been ripe for the picking for some time, and Halleck allowed Grant to be the commander to direct a siege against it. Time was of the essence since the Union had just found out that the Confederate commander, P. G. T. Beauregard, was marching straight toward the fort with fifteen regiments. Grant needed to take the fort before these Confederate reinforcements arrived.

In February of 1862, Grant took his men to Paducah, Kentucky, which they would use as a forward outpost to launch the strike against Fort Henry. Here, he amassed twenty-three regiments, which were comprised of some seventeen thousand troops. All of these men and their equipment would be placed on riverboats to sweep down upon the fort.

One thing that gave the Union troops a serious advantage was the fact that Fort Henry was constructed on low ground. This meant that as the riverboats came downriver, the fortress could be easily bombarded. Confederate forces tried to compensate for this by establishing another fortress on the other side of the river, an outpost they dubbed Fort Heiman.

This fortress was situated a little higher up on the riverbank, but it was so poorly defended that it would prove to make very little difference. In the end, the Confederates knew they did not stand a chance and promptly surrendered on February 6th, 1862, after being waylaid by a squadron led by naval commander Andrew H. Foote.

With Fort Henry under his control, Grant then sent his troops to pacify the nearby Confederate outpost of Fort Donelson, which was farther down the Cumberland River. The fort was shelled by riverboats on February 14th. Shortly after this, on February 16th, the besieged fortress surrendered to the Union troops. This surrender helped to pave a path toward Confederate-controlled Tennessee, and it is considered one of the Union's first major breakthroughs of the war.

In the following month of March, the victorious General Grant found himself leading a robust and strong group of forty thousand troops even deeper into the Confederate strongholds of the South. Immediately under his leadership were a couple of rather colorful officers—Lew Wallace and William Tecumseh Sherman.

Sherman was a brigadier general, but he was sometimes viewed as a loose cannon by the top brass. Nevertheless, he, like Grant, would rise to the top with his daring exploits during the Civil War. Lew Wallace, on the other hand, would become famous for his later role as the governor of New Mexico and his run-ins with Billy the Kid. As these brave and unique men marched south, they became the centerpieces of the incredible drama that was about to unfold.

Chapter 8 – The Battle of Shiloh and Its Aftermath

"I have nothing to do with opinions. I deal only with armed rebellion and its aiders and abettors."

-*Ulysses S. Grant*

Grant and his men had led several successful expeditions against the Confederates by the spring of 1862, but their first real battle was just before them. This first real test presented itself on April 6th, 1862. The previous day, over forty thousand Confederate troops had made their way within Union lines. Both sides began to take potshots at each other. It was as if both sides were actively testing the mettle of the other right before the main event was about to commence.

Early the next morning, Confederate General Albert Sidney Johnston sent his troops storming into the Union line, kicking off what would be known as the Battle of Shiloh. It was named as such because it was within sight of Shiloh Church. The Confederates took the Union soldiers by surprise and are said to have come down on the Union troops like an "avalanche."

In fact, Grant was taking his first cup of coffee and enjoying some breakfast when he and his chief of staff, Colonel Joseph Webster, heard the unmistakable sound of cannon fire from farther down the river. After briefly discussing the matter, Grant put aside his breakfast and proclaimed to all within earshot, "Gentlemen, the ball is in motion. Let's be off."

By the time Grant's steamboat reached Pittsburg Landing on the Tennessee River's western bank, it was a little after nine o'clock in the morning. The battle was already well underway. Grant could hear the sounds of the battle, a steady stream of gunshots and agonized cries of grown men filling the air. The 53rd Ohio Infantry Regiment was out front, taking the brunt of the assault.

Grant managed to reach General Sherman's position at 10 a.m., but by then, the 53rd had been all but decimated. This loss forced Sherman to command the rest of the troops to take evasive action and withdraw toward the banks of the Tennessee River. Confederate General Johnston was attempting to throw everything he had at the Union troops so that they could break through the Union ranks. Grant, in the meantime, reminded his own troops that they had to hold the line at all cost. And they did.

Ulysses S. Grant was a tireless taskmaster in these efforts. He rode from one part of the defensive line to the other, encouraging soldiers to go on. At times, he more directly coerced those who proved hesitant to fight, telling them to get back to the front. Grant's superb horsemanship was no doubt on display as he daringly rode up and down the line of Union troops, dodging bullets as he went.

It is said that at one point, a staff officer, who was obviously worried about Grant's safety, tried to warn him to flee. Fearing the certain collapse of the Union line, the officer told Grant, "General, we must leave this place. It isn't necessary to stay here. If we do, we shall all be dead in five minutes." These are some pretty sobering words, to be sure, but Grant, after a pause, merely acknowledged the possibility by replying, "I guess that's so."

The Union troops were not the only ones facing the threat of sudden death. A large number of Confederate fighters were cut down as well. During the terrible melee that ensued, even Confederate General Johnston ended up getting killed. Johnston was shot in the leg, and he initially believed it just to be a trivial flesh wound. He was in discomfort but would survive—or at least so he thought.

The bullet was more than a flesh wound. It had torn through his femoral artery, and it would cause him to literally bleed to death on the spot. With his abrupt passing, the direction of the Confederate forces fell on one General Pierre Gustave Toutant-Beauregard (P. G. T. for short). Interestingly enough, Johnston and Beauregard had disagreed on the strategy prior to the attack. Beauregard had not favored waging such a risky assault.

So, after Beauregard took over, his own doubts seemed to pass to all the other troops around him, and the advance soon began to slow. The Union troops, which were initially on the run, were able to rally. In a spot dubbed the "Hornet's Nest," they fought to hold their ground.

The group of Union troops struggling to fend off the Confederates at the Hornet's Nest was being led by Benjamin Prentiss. These defenders were hit by heavy artillery, and they were practically blasted into smithereens by the Confederates. After several hours of this terrific onslaught, Prentiss was forced to acknowledge defeat. What remained of his unit were then captured and made prisoners of war.

Nevertheless, even with the capture of this division, the Confederates proved unable to further penetrate what has since been called "Grant's Last Line" of defense. Grant was questioned at the time about whether or not the Union defense would hold up, and his words would prove fairly prophetic. With the sun setting across the horizon, Grant confidently stated, "They can't break our lines tonight. It's too late. Tomorrow we shall attack them with fresh troops and drive them, of course."

The Confederates were indeed forced to call off their assault. And after this day of fighting had ended, it is said that Sherman came upon Grant sitting under a tree quietly whittling a piece of wood with a knife. Sherman reflected on the terrible battle they had just waged and remarked, "Well, Grant, we've had the devil's own day, haven't we?" Grant, unphased, shot back his quiet and completely calm response, "Yes. Lick 'em tomorrow, though."

Thousands had already died on both sides, but nevertheless, the fighting began anew the following day. With the Union Army swelled by reinforcements, they were able to push the Confederates all the way back to their base in Corinth, Mississippi. Grant and the Union had won this major engagement. But the victory itself did not really change the situation on the ground.

The Confederates were forced back to where they had already been stationed in the vicinity of Corinth, and the Union troops, for the time, remained where they had been, at Pittsburg Landing. It seemed as if many lives had been lost just for a bitter stalemate to take root. Nevertheless, Grant and company began a slow advance toward the Confederate positions in Corinth all the same.

The Battle of Shiloh saw over twenty-three thousand dead and wounded; at that point in the war, it was the bloodiest battle yet. After criticism over the high causalities at Shiloh, General Halleck wanted to be cautious. Some would say overly cautious. It has been said that during this slow crawl to Corinth, the Union Army was moving less than a mile a day. The reason for their slowness was that, every so often, Halleck had them stop and dig up trenches so that they could fall back on them if necessary.

Such a thing would have been useful if they were forced to make a hasty retreat, but at this point, the Confederates were not in any shape to launch a major offensive. Grant himself believed that the troops should just charge at Corinth all at once rather than crawling along digging trenches. He thought that the city would have easily fallen to the Union forces in just a couple of days' time. Nevertheless, they pushed on at their snail's pace.

Then, in mid-May, Grant thought he saw a means of making a breakthrough. He saw that there was a point of weakness in the

Confederate lines. Grant mentioned the opening to Halleck and tried to persuade him to send his forces to charge this weakened portion of their enemy. Halleck only treated Grant's suggestion with contempt, allegedly stating that such a thing was "too stupid" to consider.

At any rate, by May 30th, Corinth was finally in sight. But by the time the Union troops had arrived, the Confederates were already making their getaway. Upon arrival, the Union soldiers were confronted not with Confederate soldiers but merely makeshift dummies the Confederates had made and put in place the day before. These dummies were like scarecrows. Old, tattered uniforms had been stuffed with hay and put on guard to face their frustrated foes. The Union had taken Corinth, but the men did not have much of a victory to show for their efforts.

However, the retreating Confederates were not far away, and Grant believed that the cavalry could easily intercept them. To his chagrin, Halleck absolutely refused to entertain this notion. The cautious Halleck must have thought that such a thing was "too stupid" to consider as well.

Ulysses S. Grant and company were now forced to sit tight on this unattractive stretch of trench-surrounded terrain. Grant was growing tired of the friction he was experiencing with General Halleck, and he actually requested to take some time off. However, he was convinced by Sherman not to do so. Sherman and Grant had become quite close during the last few months of fighting, and Sherman could not stand the thought of Grant leaving now. With some effort, Sherman was ultimately able to convince Grant to stay right where he was.

In the meantime, Grant received some major news from Washington. Halleck was being summoned to DC to take over for George McClellan. He would become the general in chief. Grant would take over as the top dog of the Union forces in the Western Theater.

In the immediate aftermath of Shiloh, Grant was widely hailed as a heroic commander. But once it sunk in with the public just how horribly high the casualty rate was, opinions began to change. Shortly thereafter, many newspaper outlets began to criticize Ulysses S. Grant for the high mortality rate, and some even accused him of being drunk at the time. Some in the press seized upon this, ridiculing General Ulysses S. Grant as a drunk who did not really know what he was doing.

Grant said very little about the criticism, but his father could not remain quiet. He was disturbed by the attacks being launched against his son, and he actually wrote to several of the major papers, demanding for them to cease their criticism. Grant did not take kindly to his father standing up for him. He had to remind his dad that he was an adult who could defend himself, and he asked him to just let the matter drop.

Embarrassed by his dad's efforts to defend him, Grant told his father, "I have not an enemy in the world who has done me so much injury in your efforts at my defense. I require no defenders and for my sake let me alone. Do nothing to correct what you have already done, but for the future keep quiet upon this subject." Grant was indeed worried about the criticism, but he continued to keep his head down. And soon, the worst of the storm had passed.

Chapter 9 – The Taking of Vicksburg

"I have never advocated war—except as a means of peace."

-Ulysses S. Grant

After the capture of Corinth and receiving his promotion, Grant took up residence in Memphis, Tennessee. Although the city was now in Union hands, its residents were most certainly not showing any "Southern hospitality" to the occupying Northerners. In fact, the local people were occasionally openly hostile. Nevertheless, Grant was able to settle in. And not only that, he was even able to have Julia and their children come to stay with him as well.

They came along right around Independence Day. Grant and company made sure that July 4th, 1862, was one to remember, with fireworks in the air and festivity on the ground. Shortly thereafter, Grant decided to move back to Corinth. There, he was able to procure one of the nicest homes in town.

He was given the house of a wealthy local by the name of Francis E. Whitfield, who had been caught sending mail to Confederate operatives. This caused him to get arrested by the Union authorities. Whitfield was then asked to take an oath of loyalty to the Union, but he refused to do so. This defiance bought him a ticket to a holding cell in Alton, Illinois. Grant moved into the detained man's home and used it as a temporary headquarters. Julia and the kids followed. They arrived by rail from Memphis shortly after Grant had procured the house.

All seemed well and good until Grant's father, Jesse, decided he had a problem with his grandkids taking up shelter in what he termed to be a rough-and-tumble army camp full of rough-and-tumble men. Grant had to write his father back to explain to him that he and his family were not actually sleeping in some tent with a bunch of drunken troops. Grant wrote the old man, "They are not running around camp among all sorts of people, but we are keeping house in the property of a truly loyal secessionist who has been furnished free board and lodging at Alton, Illinois; here the children see nothing but the greatest propriety."

Everything was relatively calm at Ulysses S. Grant's new residence, but there were some instances in which Grant witnessed bouts of chaos from his own troops. On one occasion, he was standing with his staff officers when he heard the sound of women screaming. Grant went out to investigate and saw the source of the commotion. To his horror, one of his own Union soldiers was chasing after a couple of local residents—a mother and daughter—waving his musket in the air as he pursued them.

Grant was not sure what the troublemaker was up to, but he knew it must not have been good. Grant rushed toward the soldier, grabbed the man's weapon right out of his hands, and then proceeded to beat the man over the head with his own firearm. The delinquent soldier was knocked out from the exchange, prompting an aide to remark, "I guess you have killed him, General." To which Grant gruffly replied, "If I have, it has only served him right." If Ulysses S. Grant hated anything, he hated the sight of innocent civilians being bullied by occupying troops. Any time he saw an instance of it, he was sure to respond.

However, Grant would soon have more to worry about than his own disorderly troops. He received word that Confederate General Sterling Price was bringing Confederate troops in the vicinity of the town of Iuka, Mississippi, which was some twenty miles southeast of Corinth. It seemed as if he was readying them to smash into the Union positions in northern Mississippi.

Grant was concerned about these developments, and it has been said that he spent most of the following evening pouring over all of the latest bits of information about the enemy movements on the field. Grant was certain that the Confederates were attempting to launch a major offensive in the hopes that they could deal a decisive blow against the Union Army. As the days wore on, it was then determined that Price was most likely coordinating with another Confederate commander by the name of Earl Van Dorn.

It seemed that Price might be trying to draw Union troops away from Corinth so that Van Dorn could launch a separate attack against the town. After several days of brainstorming, by September, Grant had developed his game plan. He decided that they would have to deliver a two-pronged assault that would take out the forces led by Price while simultaneously taking on the troops of Van Dorn.

Grant arranged to have one regiment led by a certain Edward Ord sent to take on the Confederates at Iuka while having another contingent under the guidance of William S. Rosecrans tackle the rest. However, once this plan was executed, there was almost immediately a problem. Heavy rains came down and slowed the march of Rosecrans's troops. Nevertheless, Grant believed that Edward Ord's troops might be able to delay Price long enough to make up for it.

In the meantime, on September 18th, Grant and his men had received news that there had been a Union victory in Sharpsburg, Maryland, against Robert E. Lee's famed Army of Northern Virginia. Grant had Ord send this news off to Price in the hopes that it might pressure the Confederate to surrender. Price refused, though, making it clear that such things made no difference to him.

At any rate, on September 19th, Rosecrans and his men reached Iuka and engaged the enemy. The Confederates proved too strong for him, and Rosecrans and company had to pull back. The Confederates then withdrew from their positions on September 20th. Although the enemy had gotten away, their advance was halted, and they were clearly defeated in battle.

Grant was also assured that Corinth had been secured. However, the fighting would erupt again just north of Corinth on October 3rd, but after two days of terrific warfare, the forces of both Van Dorn and Price were soundly defeated. Grant was disappointed, though, because a large group of Rebels was once again allowed to retreat. They fled back to their strongholds in Mississippi.

Grant would later remark in disappointment and disgust, "I cannot see how the enemy are to escape without losing everything but their small arms." But yet, once again, they did indeed slip away. Nevertheless, the war went on. On October 25th, 1862, Grant took over the command of the entire District of Tennessee. With this new command came a new headquarters, and Grant and his family ended up moving into a new home in the quaint but charming little town of La Grange that November.

Grant's next objective would be to go on the offensive and drive the Confederates out of a little-known place called Vicksburg. Vicksburg was a Confederate stronghold situated farther south on the east bank of the Mississippi River. If the Union troops could gain control of the fortress at Vicksburg, they would have control of the entire Mississippi River.

The Union troops would first converge on the nearby settlement of Holly Springs. They expected a fight, but the Confederates actually evacuated the place on November 9th. As such, when the Union troops arrived a few days later on the 13th, they found it all but deserted. Always on the move, Grant then held council with Sherman on November 21st in Columbus, Kentucky, before returning to his headquarters.

He was indeed a man on the march, going from this place to that. As he told his father in a written letter at the time, "I will again be in motion. I feel every confidence of success but I know that a heavy force is now to my front." Along with his concerns over the upcoming operation against the Confederates, Grant was also increasingly worried about the actions of the occupying Union troops under his command. After a particularly bad spate of incidences of harassment conducted by his own men, Grant was heard to remark, "Houses have been plunder'd and burned down, fencing destroyed and citizens frightened without enquiry as to their status in the Rebellion."

Having an occupying army camped out in your neighborhood is never an easy thing to deal with. It is even more difficult when the average citizen is being judged on whether or not they were loyal to the occupiers—it created an understandably toxic atmosphere. Grant was ready to rein in these trespasses, reminding his troops that any violators of the common peace would be dealt with and prosecuted accordingly. All the same, sabotage conducted by Southern sympathizers was a real threat, and Grant had to keep a constant eye out for this as well.

Grant's trusty fellow General William Tecumseh Sherman would take on the Confederates just north of Vicksburg at a place called Chickasaw Bayou on December 29th, 1862. However, the operation did not go well, and the Confederate commander, Lieutenant General John C. Pemberton, ended up pushing Sherman's group back.

However, Union General John Alexander McClernand was able to connect with Sherman's battered troops. With some effort, they managed to seize the enemy fortress—Fort Hindman—in early January of 1863. Grant appeared on the scene in Memphis on January 10th. McClernand had taken the initiative at Fort Hindman, and once Grant found out, he was infuriated. Grant wanted all the forces to focus on Vicksburg and felt that the seizure of Fort Hindman was an unnecessary distraction.

In fact, Ulysses S. Grant was so upset that he sent off a dispatch to Halleck, declaring that the rogue McClernand had "gone on a wild goose chase." Grant then sent a message to McClernand himself, ordering him, "Unless you are acting under authority not derived from me keep your command where it can soonest be assembled for the renewal of the attack on Vicksburg."

Sherman, while under the command of McClernand, carried out a successful attack on Fort Hindman a short time later, on January 12th. This victory gained a fortress as well as some five thousand Confederate prisoners of war. After this achievement, Grant received a cable from Halleck, which suggested that he should take over for General McClernand. Halleck stated, "You are hereby authorized to relieve General McClernand from command of the expedition against Vicksburg, giving it to the next in rank, or taking it yourself."

This was exactly what Grant wanted to hear. He would now lead the charge in the offensive of Vicksburg. Grant mobilized his forces and had them set up shop in a place called Milliken's Bend in Louisiana. This town was about twenty miles northwest of Vicksburg, so it made for an excellent staging area for the coming Union invasion. The biggest hardship of this spot was the fact that the site was surrounded by water.

Vicksburg itself is said to have been positioned some two hundred feet high over the Mississippi. It was nestled on a bluff that was situated on the east side of that great river. Here, it is said that the Mississippi takes a sharp turn, encompassing Vicksburg. This puts Vicksburg in a prime position for defense since artillery can be swung around at all points of approach. Having said that, it was realized that while heavily armored attack ships could sneak by, they would not be able to engage in a direct assault on the battlements.

A land invasion would be difficult as well since much of the terrain was treacherous swamplands. Grant would spend the next several weeks trying to find a way to break through to Vicksburg. He finally determined to send a daring squadron of craft shepherded by ironclad gunboats racing across the river past the Vicksburg artillery. They were supposed to land just south of Vicksburg. Since all of Vicksburg's guns were aimed at the river, once this dangerous waterway was traversed, a march through the "back door" of Vicksburg would be relatively easy by comparison.

This squadron was led by naval commander David Dixon Porter on April 16th, 1863. In the end, only one ship was lost. The boats, which were stocked full of ammunition and other supplies, safely crossed through this dangerous gauntlet with their ironclad gunboat escorts. On April 17th, Ulysses S. Grant ordered Colonel Benjamin H Grierson to launch a daring raid that would tear into Confederate positions at Jackson, Mississippi. He would then march all the way to Baton Rouge, Louisiana, thereby creating a great distraction for the Confederate forces.

In the meantime, Grant and the land invasion forces were on the move. By April 29th, they were near that so-called "backdoor" to Vicksburg with an army of forty thousand men. They were some twenty miles south of the fortress and heading north. The plan was going off without a hitch. Grant would attack Vicksburg from the south while the guns were facing in the opposite direction toward the river. The Confederate land forces were being diverted to Baton Rouge because of Colonel Grierson's simultaneously coordinated attack.

Grant launched an all-out assault on Vicksburg on May 22nd, 1863, but faced stiffer resistance than he had anticipated and temporarily had to back away. Even so, Vicksburg was surrounded by Union troops, and Grant realized it was just a matter of time before the besieged fortress would be forced to surrender. This realization was confirmed on June 28th when Grant received some inside information from a few Rebel deserters. They informed the Union troops that there was only enough food at the fort to sustain the defenders for a few more days at most.

And sure enough, on July 1st, the captain of the fort, John C. Pemberton, agreed to cease hostilities. The final terms of Vicksburg's surrender were then worked out on July 3rd, 1863. With Vicksburg's surrender complete, Grant was handed over some 32,000 prisoners of war and 172 pieces of artillery. Grant's great victory came just in time for that year's Independence Day celebration. And when Washington, DC, learned of these happenings the following day, on July 4th, it was indeed a cause for celebration.

This news, coupled with the deflection of George Pickett's charge at Gettysburg on July 3rd, made it clear to all concerned that the tide had turned. After so much bloodshed and struggle, the war was winnable. The Union was confident that it could win this war; it was now just a matter of how long it might take to do so.

Chapter 10 – The Civil War Comes to an End

"In every battle there comes a times when both sides consider themselves beaten, then he who continues the attack wins."

-Ulysses S. Grant

Ulysses S. Grant's success at Vicksburg was a stunning achievement, and unlike Shiloh, the remarks on the battle would be positive. President Lincoln and even Grant's old agitator, General Halleck, had kind words to say about Grant's leadership. Grant was given yet another promotion, becoming a major general. And if that wasn't enough, on October 16th, 1863, he was given command over the entire Division of the Mississippi. This meant that Grant had jurisdiction over the entire Western Theater of the war.

Grant was now in his early forties, and with such a high rank in the US Army, that meant he was basically set for life. The rank came with a salary of some $6,000 a year, which in those days was a lot of money, considering the fact that a regular low-ranking soldier in the Union Army, on average, made less than $600 a year.

But all accolades aside, Grant was ready to further wage war. The Union forces had been recently repelled during the Battle of

Chickamauga, and after a tactical withdrawal, the Union battalion dubbed the Army of the Cumberland were forced to hole up in Chattanooga. Union Major General Joseph Hooker led a contingent of troops to relieve the besieged fighters. Once the Army of the Cumberland was freed, Grant had General Sherman lead the Army of the Tennessee and join forces with them so they could march on Confederate positions at Missionary Ridge.

Fierce fighting erupted on November 23rd, 1863, when Union troops led by Major General George Henry Thomas came upon Confederates positioned to the north of the ridge, which was some distance south of Chattanooga. The Confederates were not prepared to face the Union soldiers and immediately retreated back to Missionary Ridge. Union troops then dug into place at a spot called Orchard Knob and prepared to launch an assault on Missionary Ridge itself.

In the meantime, General Sherman was preparing his troops to cross the Tennessee River to bolster the Union assault on Missionary Ridge. The following day, on November 24th, Sherman's group stalled and was unable to advance in time. Another Union general—Joseph Hooker—managed to seize a strategic position on Lookout Mountain, which allowed the Union to jump out in front of the Confederate lines.

Grant ordered Thomas to charge the Confederate positions at Missionary Ridge on the 25th. After a complicated, coordinated effort, in which Thomas took much initiative, the Confederates were defeated. The Union troops had thereby managed to gain dominance over all of Tennessee and had a clear path to march on the Confederate stronghold of Georgia. Grant would end up spending the winter in Nashville, Tennessee, and Julia would stay with him.

During her time in Nashville, Grant's wife began to volunteer at the army hospital, tending to the many wounded soldiers. Seeing all of these wounded men really made an impression on her about the true cost of the war. But whenever she mentioned her experiences at the hospital to Grant, he did not seem to want to hear much about it. In fact, Grant is said to have told her on one occasion, "Now, my dear, I don't want to hear anything about that. I don't want you to come to me with any of these tales of the hospitals. I have all I can bear up under outside my home, and when I come to you I want to see you and the children and talk about other matters. I want to get all the sunshine I can."

Grant was a pragmatic and practical man. He understood the horrors of war, but he also understood the necessity of not dwelling on such things while one was in the midst of a terrible conflict. Like many military men, past and present, Grant had learned to compartmentalize some of the more difficult aspects of his life.

Although Nashville is a Southern city, the winter of 1863/64 proved to be a cold one. And this, along with Grant's occasionally chilly disposition, prompted Julia to leave Nashville for the "warmer" climate of St. Louis. Ulysses S. Grant was left to his own machinations in the spring of 1864, and he deeply contemplated how the war was shaping up.

Grant received word on March 2nd that President Abraham Lincoln had given him yet another promotion, this time to lieutenant general. This was a major advancement, as it essentially gave Grant the ability to direct the Union Army as a whole. Grant left for DC shortly thereafter.

There is a story that Grant arrived at the prestigious Willard Hotel on March 8th, 1864. He was accompanied by his fourteen-year-old son, Fred, and he was initially unrecognized by the clerk. Grant, who had eschewed ostentatious, decorated uniforms ever since a local troublemaker in Ohio mocked him after his graduation from West Point, did not dress to impress. In fact, his wrinkled, standard-issue uniform made him look like some dingy, run-of-the-mill soldier.

But after Grant signed his name at the front desk, the clerk began singing a different tune and attempted to offer him the best room in the house. After Grant checked in and tucked his tired child into bed, he came back down to the lobby, where he was greeted by a throng of curious well-wishers. Just like today, word in Washington travels fast.

Eventually, however, Grant was able to make his way over to the White House, where President Lincoln was waiting for him. Grant was directed to the East Room, where a reception had been arranged for him. Lincoln himself strode right up to Grant, took him by the hand, and led him over to the First Lady who was waiting nearby and remarked, "Why look, Mother—here is General Grant."

Lincoln had indeed heard much of the war hero, and he was thrilled to finally have his winning general standing before him. The pair made a striking contrast physically, with Grant being short and slightly stout while Lincoln was tall and trim. Ulysses S. Grant, whose habitual slouching made him appear even shorter than his five feet, seven inches frame otherwise would have conveyed, was so short that, at one point, Lincoln had him stand up on a couch. This was done so that others in the room could have a better look at the great victor of Vicksburg.

There was plenty of small talk, but the serious discussions came later that night when Lincoln sat down privately with Grant to have a word with him. The most important thing that the president covered was the level of autonomy and authority that he was giving Grant. Some presidents, even to this day, would prefer to be in the driver's seat as the commander in chief and dictate to their generals what to do. Others have a more hands-off style in which they delegate authority to their most trusted subordinates and allow them to make important decisions themselves.

Lincoln made it clear to Grant that he trusted him enough to think for himself. President Lincoln assured General Grant that he had full confidence in his ability to lead the troops and would leave the most immediate decisions on the field for him to decide. The next day, Grant was given his commission in a formal ceremony at which Lincoln was present.

In his acceptance speech, Ulysses S. Grant's words, like usual, were brief, modest, and to the point. To Lincoln and everyone else who had gathered to hear him speak, Grant remarked, "Mr. President: I accept this commission with gratitude for the high honor conferred. With the aid of the noble armies that have fought on so many fields for our common country, it will be my earnest endeavor not to disappoint your expectations. I feel the full weight of the responsibilities now devolving on me and know that if they are met it will be due to those armies, and above all to the favor of that Providence which leads both nations and men."

After leaving DC, Grant set up a new headquarters in nearby Culpepper, Virginia, where he would preside over General George Meade's Army of the Potomac. Due to the wide availability of the telegraph, Grant did not intend to stay in one spot for long. As Grant wistfully remarked in a letter to his father at the time, "In these days of telegraphy and steam I can command whilst traveling and visiting about."

Yes, the ability to hop on a train to receive updates of various positions on the field from telegraph posts all along the tracks certainly changed the way in which a war could be run. But if Grant thought he would be free to move as he pleased, he would find this to be more wishful thinking than reality.

Nevertheless, Grant would orchestrate the greatest battle yet to come—an attack on Robert E. Lee's formidable Army of Northern Virginia. In early May, Grant led a contingent of troops across the Rapidan River, and they began to make their way farther south. The group then found themselves in wilderness-like conditions, as they had to march across rugged terrain.

Lee did not try to hinder the crossing of Union troops over the Rapidan. But as soon as they were on this rough, uneven ground, Lee decided to let them have it. Grant and company were immediately repulsed off the main roads and forced to take shelter in the surrounding woods. Many in the Union—and most likely the

Confederate-Army thought that Grant should retreat back across the river, but he refused.

Instead, he urged his men to engage in an all-out assault the following day. Grant's group sustained heavy casualties, but Grant refused to give up. Later that evening, he and his troops moved under cover of darkness to Lee's rightmost flank and then south behind Confederate lines. Lee was initially taken aback by this outflanking maneuver, but he quickly recovered and rapidly sent his troops to confront the Union forces near the site of Spotsylvania.

Here, the fighting bitterly continued from May 8th all the way until May 20th, with both sides delivering a blistering barrage. It was brutal, but Grant refused to give up. He actually fired off a note to General Halleck on May 11th, in which he plainly stated his determination, declaring, "I propose to fight it out on this line if it takes all summer." But as the dead and wounded continued to pile up, the specter of that bloody Battle of Shiloh began to return.

It has been said that at this point, the Union may have lost as many as eighteen thousand troops, whereas the Confederates had lost around twelve thousand. Even though the losses were greater on the Union side, the Confederate losses were more painful since they had a much more limited pool of troops to rely on.

Although it was true the Union was better equipped to raise troops, that did not mean that soldiers were expendable enough to be herded through meat grinders. The word "butcher" began to be leveled at Grant by some of his own subordinates behind his back. Nevertheless, Grant was determined to continue.

Grant once again attempted an outflanking maneuver, but Lee was too quick and immediately responded to counteract it. This led to another bloody day of close, brutal combat between both sides. However, Robert E. Lee's army was quickly losing steam, and by June, he and his men were forced to make a tactical retreat to Richmond. Ulysses S. Grant and the Union Army remained in hot pursuit, with the Union forces coming as close as six miles to Richmond by June 2nd.

Lee knew that he could not sustain any more heavy losses, so he decided to hunker down in Richmond and prepare for a standoff. Lee had trenches dug and fortifications erected as he waited for a final clash with the Union. On the following day, Grant ordered a full-frontal assault on the Confederate positions. However, the Union troops were unable to break the Confederate lines, so a new strategy was needed.

Shifting gears, Grant led his army across the James River on June 14th and attempted to take the town of Petersburg, which was situated just south of Richmond. Petersburg was defended by a force of some 1,500 troops led by Confederate General P. G. T. Beauregard.

Grant's Union contingent easily outnumbered this group, but Beauregard's forces fought so ferociously that they held off long enough for Lee to rush over with what was left of the Army of Northern Virginia. Grant's weary troops were not ready for another large clash, so the two sides ended up settling into yet another protracted standoff.

In the midst of this intensity, Ulysses S. Grant had his army engineers construct what has been termed a veritable "city of wooden huts." In the center of all of this was Grant's headquarters, from which he would command his massive army. Incredibly enough, despite the nature of the war zone, Grant had considered the status quo of the stalemate stable enough and had his wife and children come join him as he oversaw the siege's progress.

The base camp that was constructed was impressive, and its very existence, along with the overwhelming advantage of Union numbers, would make a visitor to the encampment wonder why the stalemate even existed. Grant, for one, would have been quick to point out the reason—the Confederates had the edge over them due to their interior lines. This means that as long as the Confederates had control of the innermost part of their battlements, they could have reinforcements—

as meager as they might have been—quickly rushed off to one side or the other in the advent of a sudden Union charge. So, even if they were outnumbered, the Union troops would face a bloody battle upon their approach.

Grant knew this well enough, and it was for this reason that he was willing to wait the Confederates out before attempting another full-frontal assault. This point was perfectly illustrated by an incident that occurred in July, in which one of the Union engineers managed to dig under the Confederate defensive positions and plant a mine. The mine blew up a short time later, killing hundreds of Confederate troops.

Right after this, the Union troops attempted to charge into the site where the bomb had gone off, but as soon as they did, the Confederates quickly reacted. They let loose with a wild barrage of gunfire, killing many of the Union troops who charged forward. The situation was so bad that some described it as being akin to "shooting fish in a barrel."

The Confederates must have known deep down that the battle was ultimately theirs to lose. They knew that even if the Union pulled back and resorted to slowly chipping away at them rather than engaging in a full-on assault, it would be just a matter of time. And General Ulysses S. Grant knew that the main objective had been accomplished; it was just a matter of fulfilling it.

In the meantime, he had all manner of visitors come to pay him his respects right there on the battlefield. Along with his wife and children, none other than President Abraham Lincoln stopped by, arriving by steamboat. One of these meetings was actually captured by a photographer, depicting Lincoln and Grant in the midst of conversation, although in the image you might not know it. In that particular frame, the two appear to be sharing a quiet, somber moment with serious expressions on their faces.

It was not until April of 1865 that the siege finally began to break. The dwindling Confederate forces realized that they could no longer sustain their positions near Richmond. When Confederate President Jefferson Davis fled from the capital of the Confederacy on April 2nd, General Lee and the surviving Confederate forces followed suit, heading off to Lynchburg, Virginia.

Richmond was now firmly in Union hands, and the rest of the South would soon follow. All that remained was to force General Robert E. Lee to surrender what remained of the tattered Army of Northern Virginia. Grant sought to do this without wasting any more bullets. Instead of firing off weapons, he fired off a letter to Lee, beseeching him to give up. Here is Grant's letter to Lee in full:

"The results of the last week must convince you of the hopelessness of further resistance on the part of the Army of Northern Virginia in this struggle. I feel that it is so, and regard it as my duty to shift from myself the responsibility of any further effusion of blood, by asking of you the surrender of that portion of the Confederate States army known as the Army of Northern Virginia."

Lee immediately responded back, and he was very careful with his words. He acknowledged the desperation but tried to make things better than they were by stating that he was "not entertaining the opinion you express on the hopelessness of further resistance." At the same time, though, Lee faced reality enough to agree that it was also his "desire to avoid a useless effusion of blood."

It was this understanding that would lead these two men from opposing sides of the war to meet at Virginia's now-famous Appomattox Court House on April 9th, 1865. Here, these two men who had served together as comrades some twenty years prior in the Mexican-American War met as the leaders of two opposing armies. The meeting of the two men is said to have been gracious enough, and after a quick expenditure of pleasantries, the two generals hammered out the terms that would finally end the American Civil War.

Grant, of course, insisted on a full and unconditional surrender, but he was forgiving enough to allow the Southern fighters a road back to normalcy. Rather than locking them all up as prisoners of war, Grant stipulated that the Confederate troops could be placed on a conditional form of parole. Grant's written directive stated that these former Confederates were "not to be disturbed by U.S. authority so long as they observe their paroles and the laws in force where they may reside."

The terms were generous enough for the battered and weary Confederate General Robert E. Lee, and he approved of them, signing his name to the agreement. Ulysses S. Grant felt so strongly about rehabilitating the Southerners who had rebelled that he even ordered his troops not to rejoice at their victory in order to avoid further animosity between them and their vanquished opponents.

The forty-two-year-old General Grant was trying hard to put the pieces of the country back together, but a terrible event would occur just days later that would make the nation once again feel as if it had been torn asunder. On April 14th, 1865, President Abraham Lincoln would be shot. He would die the very next morning.

Chapter 11 – Grant's Role as Lincoln's Successor

"I suffer the mortification of seeing myself attacked right and left by people at home professing patriotism and love of country who have never heard the whistle of a hostile bullet. I pity them and the nation dependent on such for its existence. I am thankful, however that, though such people make a great noise, the masses are not like them."

-Ulysses S. Grant

Ulysses S. Grant, like much of the rest of the country, was absolutely shocked by what had happened to Abraham Lincoln. But even more shocking for Grant was the circumstances surrounding the event. As all of the history books tell us, President Lincoln was shot at Ford's Theatre during an evening in which he, his wife, and other close associates were enjoying some much-needed rest.

Everyone was intently watching the play unfold on stage when Confederate zealot and well-known actor John Wilkes Booth took the spotlight from the stage. He entered Lincoln's box, shot the president in the head, and jumped on the stage, shouting, "Sic semper tyrannis!"

Prior to attending this event, Lincoln had held a cabinet meeting that very day in which Grant was in attendance. After the cabinet meeting dispersed, Lincoln took Grant aside and invited him and his wife to attend that very production at Ford Theatre later that night. Grant was not sure if he could make it, but he conferred with his wife. Julia said she had other plans and told her husband that she was taking their son Jesse with her to Burlington that evening.

This gave Grant the perfect excuse not to attend, and Lincoln, with his natural patience and understanding nature, told Grant that was perfectly fine. One must wonder, of course, what might have transpired if Grant was seated beside Lincoln when the assassin's bullet struck. Ulysses S. Grant himself certainly must have wondered.

At any rate, Ulysses and Julia had just gotten off at a train station in Philadelphia when a telegram was rushed over to Grant informing him of what happened. It has been said that the blood appeared to drain from Ulysses S. Grant's face as he realized that the president had been shot. Lincoln was not yet dead at this point, but it was clear to all involved that it was a mortal injury.

Grant, like many, shared a dark and desperate sentiment. The nation had finally been led through the terrible civil war only to see the man who led them through it perish. Abraham Lincoln, who had been reelected in 1864, was the one everyone thought would rebuild the nation after the war ended, yet that hope was dashed.

After his passing, President Lincoln's funeral was held on April 19th, 1865, and General Ulysses S. Grant was there, overseeing the ceremony. Grant was largely known for being stoic and unemotional, but on this sad day, he did not hold back and was seen openly crying.

With Lincoln's death, his vice president, Andrew Johnson, took over, which was a prospect that Grant was not too thrilled about. Grant knew that the true way to rebuild the country was to follow Lincoln's approach of leniency toward the Southerners. He knew that a harsh peace would only prolong hostilities and internal discord. Grant feared that Johnson might upend his and Lincoln's efforts of reconciliation by exacting draconian measures against the Southerners.

However, shortly into President Johnson's administration, Grant began to warm up to the presidential newcomer. At one point, he is said to have remarked, "I have every reason to hope that in our new President we will find a man disposed and capable of conducting the government in its old channel."

Grant wanted the continuity of Lincoln's agenda more than anything, but Johnson would ultimately disappoint him on this front. The two men would come to blows over Johnson's harshness on June 7th, 1865, when Grant famously defended his former adversary Robert E. Lee. President Johnson had Lee indicted by a grand jury for his rebellion and was ready to have Lee executed on charges of the "high crime of treason against the United States."

In Johnson's hard line against the Rebels, he wanted to make Lee an example to others. Grant was horrified at these developments and immediately made his way to the White House to tell President Johnson that Lee's life should be secure under the agreement that he had made with Lee at that Appomattox Court House at the end of the war.

In fact, Grant was so enraged that he told President Johnson he would quit rather than see Lee prosecuted. This finally prompted Johnson to reconsider, and the charges against Robert E. Lee were ultimately dropped. It was not the first time that the two men would clash. Another terrible exchange emerged in August of 1867 after Johnson fired the secretary of war, Edwin Stanton, and made Grant the interim secretary.

Grant did not approve of Stanton's dismissal, but he felt it was his duty to comply, so he filled the new role. This was not the end of the story, though. President Johnson's overreach had never been approved by the Senate. This resulted in Congress voting to bring Stanton back in December of 1867. Edwin Stanton was then officially placed back in his position on January 10th, 1868.

Grant realized the bind he was in, and he informed Johnson that he needed to quit the role of secretary of war in order to follow procedure. Johnson disagreed and argued that he would be able to overturn the results. He urged Grant to stay on board. Nevertheless, a short time later, Grant made good on his threat to quit and resigned. Johnson was infuriated with Grant, feeling that he had betrayed him. During an emotionally charged cabinet meeting, he actually went on to denounce Grant as untrustworthy, speaking at length of his supposed duplicity.

All of these shenanigans would lead to President Andrew Johnson's own impeachment. Johnson would end up beating impeachment but just barely—he avoided it by just a single vote. Despite all of the chaos, Grant was not viewed as a bad character in all this. Grant was viewed as an honorable stalwart of the rule of law, which means he was far from being seen as being duplicitous.

Grant had long been considered a potential contender for the presidency, and the grace and character that he had presented through this political storm only helped his star to rise. This was why in the election of 1868, Grant became a shoo-in for becoming the next Republican candidate for president. And sure enough, at the 1868 Republican National Convention held in Chicago that year, Grant was nominated to be at the top of the ticket for the party.

Ulysses S. Grant was a reluctant candidate, but he also felt a strong conviction that this could be his opportunity to make sure that Abraham Lincoln's legacy was followed. Grant ultimately won the election, receiving 214 electoral college votes compared to his opponent—Horatio Seymour's—80 votes. He was sworn into office on March 4th, 1869. The forty-six-year-old Ulysses S. Grant was now ready for a new title—President of the United States.

Upon becoming president, one of the first major pieces of legislation that Grant championed was the Fifteenth Amendment. This amendment to the US Constitution sought to give every male citizen "regardless of race, color, or previous condition of servitude" the right to vote. It is worth noting that this amendment did not give *women* the right to vote—only males. Women would not be given the right to vote until 1920.

Another achievement of Grant's presidency was the Ku Klux Klan Act of 1871, which sought to shut down the Southern-spawned terrorist organization that had been intimidating and terrorizing the post-Civil War South. Prior to this act, such crimes were handled at the local level, with very few meaningful results. This bit of legislation allowed the federal government as a whole to go after dangerous domestic groups such as the Ku Klux Klan (KKK).

This was especially important as it pertained to the Ku Klux Klan since the KKK was established in the South as a violent group hellbent on repressing recently freed slaves, as well as other minorities. Grant knew all too well that the crimes of the KKK would never be rightfully prosecuted by the Southern legislatures. Grant knew that it would take a federal law to prosecute and bring the Klan members to justice. And his 1871 act was efficient in doing so.

A much less successful measure taken by Grant was his attempt to annex San Domingo or, as it is known today, the Dominican Republic. Grant argued hard for the annexation and tried to push for it in both 1870 and 1871, but the measure fell through both times. Part of Grant's reasoning for making San Domingo a state was to provide a potential safe haven for some of the recently freed African Americans of the South.

Grant also had his fair share of controversy, starting with the Crédit Mobilier scandal, which erupted in the middle of his administration in the fall of 1872. This scandal saw members of Congress engaging in insider trading. An official congressional investigation was launched, and two members of Congress were censured. President Grant himself was not directly implicated, but the scandal damaged his reputation. Nevertheless, Grant would be reelected that same year, even though the scandal would continue to swirl around his second term in office.

In 1873, shortly after he was sworn in for his next four years, the nation faced a severe economic depression. And the way that this depression was brought on was in itself a scandal. It was centered around the New York-based brokerage firm Jay Cooke and Company. Jay Cooke was an up-and-coming businessman and banker who had taken the initiative during the Civil War to buy war bonds. These operations quickly increased Cooke's prestige, and by the end of the war, he could proudly say that he had been an integral part of financing the Union effort.

After the war had ended, Cooke began to become involved with the financial operations of another juggernaut—the Northern Pacific Railway. This massive railway would span some two thousand miles from the country's midsection all the way to the western coast on the Pacific.

Needless to say, such an operation requires a lot of money, and it needed government grants in order to be completed—including land grants. Cooke ended up greasing the palms of several politicians in order to get the necessary legislation passed that enabled the allocation of millions of acres to be set aside for rail lines for the Northern Pacific. Cooke also shelled out a lot of money to the Republican National Committee to make sure that Grant was reelected in 1872.

Cooke also ran his own bank, of which Grant himself had been a customer. Ulysses S. Grant knew Cooke on a personal level, and he had even visited him at his home in Philadelphia. Grant was actually staying over at Cooke's house in September of 1873 when he received word that the Northern Pacific Railway's stocks had crashed. Cooke's own bank was the number one shareholder, so this obviously presented a big problem for him.

Nevertheless, Cooke put on a brave face before Grant and acted as if everything would be fine. However, by the time Grant got back to the White House, he was made aware of just how devastating the failure of the Northern Pacific would be. Grant was not the most astute economist, but he knew enough to realize that with such a major institution going under, a financial panic might be on the horizon.

And soon, he had to turn his attention to his secretary of the treasury—W. D. Richardson—who was attempting to prevent an all-out economic collapse. Widespread paper currency or, as it was commonly known back then, "greenbacks" were still a fairly new innovation in the United States. And as such, the idea of just printing out money was new as well.

As any economist will tell you, paper money is merely a representation of value—the more you print, the less value those greenbacks represent. And the more dollars you put in circulation, the less those dollars are worth. In turn, you will find inflated prices on everything from bread to fuel. As such, it is the role of the US Treasury to try to balance these things out.

Just prior to the Northern Pacific debacle, Secretary of the Treasury Richardson had just taken some $44 million out of circulation, reducing the number of bills available to the public to just $356 million. As treasurer, it was fully within his right to remove excess paper money. But for him to introduce more money, he would need to okay it with Congress. However, Richardson was facing a crisis, so he thought he did not have to wait for a green light from Congress. Instead, he immediately put $26 million back into circulation in an attempt to offset the collapse of the Northern Pacific Railway.

These efforts fell flat, and banks and corporations were soon going under one after the other. In some ways, this disaster had a strange unifying effect in the way that only a national crisis can. As divided as the North and South may have been from the Civil War, the whole country now shared this same burden.

But at the same time, this dire shift of the economy proved somewhat disastrous to the ongoing efforts of Reconstruction in the

South. The priorities of Washington could not help but shift to the economy in general rather than rebuilding Southern institutions.

It is always a strange conundrum to fight inflation with inflation, but farmers were complaining about an inability to pay the railroad to transport their agricultural products. Congress attempted to intervene by introducing the infamous Inflation Bill. This bill would retroactively make Richardson's unilateral act of adding $26 million a part of proper protocol, and it would also add another $18 million, which bumped the total amount of bills in circulation up to $400 million.

Grant initially thought that the bill was necessary and could do some good. However, the more he contemplated the long-term effects of pumping more money into the system, the more he did not like it. And by the time the bill came to Grant's desk in the spring of 1874, he decided to veto it. Grant wrote out his thoughts at the time, stating, "It is a fair inference that if in practice this measure should fail to create the abundance of circulation expected of it, the friends of the measure, particularly those out of Congress, would clamor for [more] inflation."

In other words, Grant feared that succumbing to a supposed short-term fix of flooding the economy with more dollars would only lead to more inflation when that short-term fix proved to not be enough later on. So, with these things rattling around in his mind, Grant made up his mind to veto the bill on April 21st, 1874.

All of this political turmoil seemed to have helped Grant and his fellow Republicans lose the house in the 1874 midterm elections. Grant's own personal reputation had begun to slide as well. He was still admired as a war hero, but accusations of incompetence and even drunkenness were frequent lines of attack by his opponents.

The Democrats, who had been losing national elections since the Civil War, finally managed to win a majority in the House of Representatives. Since the Democratic Party was largely sympathetic to the former Confederacy, Democrat representatives began to push back against efforts to reform Southern institutions. Nevertheless, Grant managed to pass the robust Civil Rights Act of 1875, which sought to address some of the abuses being committed on the local level in the South. This would be the last bit of civil rights legislation passed until the Civil Rights Act of 1957 was signed by Republican President Dwight D. Eisenhower.

Unfortunately, by the time Grant's tenure in the White House came to an end in 1877, his efforts with civil rights legislation were being largely repressed by Southern legislatures and, on some notable occasions, even the Supreme Court. And by the time Grant's successor—Rutherford B. Hayes—became the next president, all efforts of Reconstruction were largely considered to be over.

At this point, Grant was not considering a third term, although he would eventually be pressured to give it some serious thought in the election of 1880. Upon his exit from the White House in 1877, he would leave the position of president to others. Having said that, Grant must not have been too pleased with how his successor, President Hayes, handled that last, sad chapter of Reconstruction.

Rutherford B. Hayes would remove the last federal troops from the South. These troops had been kept in place to safeguard the rights of African Americans and curb the abuses of Southern officials. But to please the Southerners, they were removed. In many ways, Hayes, although a Republican, became a conciliatory president and sought to appease the Democrats. The election of 1876 itself was shrouded in controversy due to widespread voting irregularities in Democrat-run states in the South.

Funnily enough, Grant's last act before leaving office involved fashioning an electoral commission to get to the bottom of allegations of fraud and irregularity in the 1876 election. After the commission determined that Hayes would be president, the Democrats began to cry foul.

To appease the Democratic Party, the Republicans established the so-called "Compromise of 1877," which had the last federal troops leaving the Democrat-run Southern states. As for Ulysses S. Grant? He was understandably worn down by all of the drama of the White House. Upon his exit in 1877, he was more than ready to start a brand-new chapter in his life.

Conclusion: The Pursuit of Perfection

If one were to sum up Grant's military and political career in the simplest of terms, it could be said that he was an eager and ready general but a very reluctant president. Shortly after he left office, he confided in a friend of his—John Russell Young—just what he thought about his post-political career. In reflection of his exit from DC, Grant declared, "I was never as happy in my life as the day I left the White House. I felt like a boy getting out of school."

After leaving the White House, Grant essentially took a long overdue vacation. He always wanted to travel overseas but had never had the chance to do so. Now was his time. He and his wife got on a boat, crossed the Atlantic, and embarked upon what would essentially become a world tour. He financed the trip with proceeds from a Nevada mining outfit that he had invested in. Grant had netted some $25,000 from the venture and spent just about all of it while he was abroad. This amounted to a small fortune in those days, yet Grant did not blink an eye.

However, Grant's trip was not just a vacation; it was a kind of an unofficial diplomatic mission that had him breaking bread with several important and powerful leaders of the day. He met with Queen

Victoria in Britain, Pope Leo XIII in Italy, Otto von Bismarck in Germany, and even Japanese Emperor Meiji in far-off Japan. During the course of his adventure, Grant made his way over to Jerusalem, becoming the first American president to visit this great focal point of the world's three major monotheistic faiths.

Even in his youth, Ulysses S. Grant always wanted to see the world. And in his old age, he did just that. The tour came to an end when Grant and company hopped on a freighter parked off the Japanese coast and made their way across the Pacific Ocean. They ended up in Ulysses S. Grant's old stomping grounds of San Francisco on September 20th, 1879.

After this long overdue "rest," which had Grant practically circumnavigating the globe, politics once again came into the picture. Republican President Rutherford B. Hayes had pledged to serve only one term, so Grant was once again propped up as a potential candidate in the 1880 election.

At this point in American history, there was no such thing as a term limit, but it was an unspoken tradition. George Washington, the first US president, thought that a president should quit after two terms. Grant quietly insisted that he would prefer not to run, but he allowed the drama to play out. In the end, his party chose a man named James A. Garfield to be their standard-bearer instead.

This no doubt served as a great relief for Grant, who was then allowed to retire from the political scene entirely. Grant spent much of the rest of his life writing his own memoirs. Sadly, he also spent his last few years seeking to prop up a series of failed business ventures. This included—perhaps ironically, considering the debacle of the Northern Pacific during his presidency—a scheme to build a railroad in Mexico.

Grant attempted to partner with the Mexican Southern Railroad to build a new rail line from the Mexican cities of Oaxaca to Mexico City. Despite his best efforts, however, the company would ultimately go bankrupt. Grant's health began to decline shortly thereafter. He quietly passed away from a prolonged battle with cancer of the esophagus on July 23rd, 1885.

He was only sixty-three years old, and he doubtless would have lived a lot longer if it was not for his lifelong adoration of cigars. Grant had picked up the habit during his military days, and despite doctor's orders, it had stuck with him for most of his life. But despite any of his foibles and bad habits—maybe even because of them—Grant was a beloved American figure.

Grant was not perfect, but he was a man who honestly tried to do his best. And upon his death, he was remembered for these great, universally appreciated virtues. And since Grant was not perfect, he realized that America was not perfect either. But nevertheless, he believed in ceaselessly striving for a "more perfect union." Ulysses S. Grant knew that perfection was merely a work in progress, and he spent his life pursuing it. In the end, he gave his country the best he could offer, and the nation could not have asked for much more.

Here's another book by Captivating History that you might like

Free Bonus from Captivating History (Available for a Limited time)

Hi History Lovers!

Now you have a chance to join our exclusive history list so you can get your first history ebook for free as well as discounts and a potential to get more history books for free! Simply visit the link below to join.

Captivatinghistory.com/ebook

Also, make sure to follow us on Facebook, Twitter and Youtube by searching for Captivating History.

Appendix A: Further Reading and References

Ulysses S. Grant: Triumph over Adversity, 1822-1865. Brooks D. Simpson. 2000.

Ulysses S. Grant: The Unlikely Hero. Michael Korda. 2004.

Ulysses S. Grant: Soldier and President. Geoffrey Perret. 1997.

Personal Memoirs of U. S. Grant. Ulysses S. Grant. 1885.

Grant. Ron Chernow. 2017.

To Rescue the Republic: Ulysses S. Grant, the Fragile Union, and the Crisis of 1876. Bret Baier & Catherine Whitney. 2021.

Made in the USA
Columbia, SC
14 February 2022